Rotary Riot
40 Fast & Fabulous Quilts

Judy Hopkins and Nancy J. Martin

Credits

Cover Photo . . . . Doug Plager
Photography . . . . Brent Kane
Illustration and Graphics . . . . Linda and
                          Chris Gentry of Artworks
Text and Cover Design . . . . Judy Petry
Editor . . . . Liz McGehee

Rotary Riot: 40 Fast and Fabulous Quilts©
©1991 by Judy Hopkins and Nancy J. Martin

That Patchwork Place, Inc.
PO Box 118, Bothell, WA 98041-0118

Printed in Singapore
96 95 94 93 92 6 5 4 3 2

Library of Congress Cataloging-in-Publication Data

Hopkins, Judy,
    Rotary Riot: 40 fast and fabulous quilts / Judy
Hopkins and Nancy J. Martin
        p. cm.
      ISBN 0-943574-86-2 :
      1. Patchwork—Patterns. 2. Cutting 3. Quilting—
Patterns.
    I. Martin, Nancy J.   II. Title
    TT835.H573 1991   91-26050
    746.9'7—dc20   CIP

Acknowledgments

Special thanks are extended to:

    Ella Bosse, Louise Bremner, Evelyn Bright, Jackie Carley, Roxanne Carter, Ramona Chinn, Mimi Dietrich, Donna Hanson Eines, Alice Graves, Leona Gordon Harleman, Peggy Hinchey, Ruth Horvath, Judy Morrison, Joyce B. Peaden, Paulette Peters, Carol Rhoades, Sheila Robinson, Terri Shinn, Cathy Shultz, Bernice Riley Smalley, Jeanie Smith, Joyce Stewart, George Taylor, and Byrd B. Tribble for providing quilts.

    Sue von Jentzen, Freda Smith, and Jean Fries' quilting service for their fine hand quilting.

    Lois Zehr and Debby Coates for the illuminating information on the Mennonite Tack.

Contents

Introduction

Quiltmaking techniques have undergone many changes since the Olfa company introduced its rotary cutter and mat in 1978. The rotary cutter was originally produced to cut sewing patterns and fabric, but quiltmakers soon adapted this handy tool to cut the geometric shapes and strips needed for their quilts. The tedious hours spent making and tracing templates were no longer necessary!

Most quiltmakers today have a basic knowledge of rotary cutting and incorporate some Template-Free™ techniques into their quilts. Strip piecing is not new. The October 1972 issue of *Quilter's Newsletter Magazine* (No. 36) featured a tree block made from strip piecing. Sally Lingwood of Anacortes, Washington, tells of using bias strip piecing with a paper template when she made her Pine Tree quilt in 1933. Ninepatches and Double Irish Chains have long been produced with a strip-piecing method.

As quiltmakers and teachers, both of us must produce a riot of samples within short deadlines. Template-Free™ quiltmaking helps us to achieve this goal while allowing time for experimentation. Not all of our quilts meet our expectations. Says Judy, "I'm only pleased with about one of every four quilts I produce. So I have a collection of tops that I sometimes use as quilt backs."

In *Rotary Riot*, we have taken forty traditional blocks that appeal to many quiltmakers and adapted their construction to Template-Free™ techniques. We begin with Nancy's basic review of rotary-cutting techniques and information on multi-fabric quilts in the front of the book.

The pattern section includes step-by-step directions for forty favorite quilts, all clearly illustrated and written in a Template-Free™ format. Some of the patterns feature bias squares, some include large blocks and triangles that are easily cut with the 8" Bias Square®, and several use simple strip-piecing techniques. The patterns are graded with symbols as to difficulty, so you can match the pattern to your skill level.

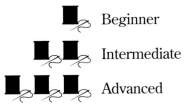

Judy has written a section on "Finishing Your Quilt" and has included some of the overall repeat quilting patterns for which she is known. Also included is information on crow footing, utility quilting, and other tacking techniques.

We have both devised special cutting guides that help us with our Template-Free™ techniques. In 1987 Nancy produced the Bias Square® cutting guide, which she uses to produce the sewn half-square triangle units called bias squares. Judy recently developed the ScrapSaver™ tool for quick-cutting half-square triangles from irregular scraps. Both tools will help you save valuable time as you use up all those interesting scraps you have accumulated. Then you'll have more time to purchase more fabric and produce more quilts to create your own "Rotary Riot."

Nancy & Judy

Materials and Supplies

Rotary Cutter and Mat

A large rotary cutter will enable you to quickly cut strips and pieces without templates. A mat with a rough finish will hold the fabric in place and protect both the blade and table on which you are cutting. An 18" x 24" mat will allow you to cut long bias strips. A smaller mat is ideal when working with scraps.

Cutting Guides

You will need a ruler for measuring and to guide the rotary cutter. There are many appropriate rulers on the market, but a favorite is the Rotary Rule™. It is made from ⅛" Plexiglas™ and includes markings for 45° and 60° angles, guidelines for cutting strips, plus the standard measurements. The Rotary Mate™ is a 12"-long cutting guide with the same features. The Bias Square® is the tool most critical to bias strip piecing. This acrylic cutting guide is available in two sizes, 6" or 8" square, and is ruled with ⅛" markings. It features a diagonal line, which is placed on the bias seam, enabling you to cut two accurately sewn half-square triangles. The Bias Square® is convenient to use when cutting small quilt pieces, such as squares, rectangles, and triangles. The larger 8" size is ideal for quick-cutting blocks that require large squares and triangles as well as making diagonal cuts for quarter-square triangles. A 20cm-square metric version is also available for those who prefer to work in this format.

The ScrapSaver™ cutting guide is a tool designed for cutting individual half-square triangles in a variety of sizes from scraps.

All of the cutting guides are available from That Patchwork Place, Inc., P.O. Box 118, Bothell, WA 98041-0118.

Sewing Machine

You need a straight-stitch machine in good working order. Make sure the tension is adjusted so that you are producing smooth, even seams. A seam that is puckered will cause the fabric to curve and will distort the size of your piecing. Use a new needle in the machine so the fabric is not snagged or distorted with thread pulls. (Old needles usually make a popping sound as they enter the fabric.)

Needles

Use sewing-machine needles sized for cotton fabrics (size 70/10 or 80/12). You will also need hand-sewing needles (Sharps) and hand-quilting needles (Betweens #8, #9, #10).

Pins

A good supply of glass- or plastic-headed pins is necessary. Long pins are especially helpful when pinning thick layers together.

Iron and Ironing Board

Frequent and careful pressing are necessary to ensure a smooth, accurately stitched quilt top. Locate your iron and ironing board, along with a plastic spray bottle of water, close to your sewing machine.

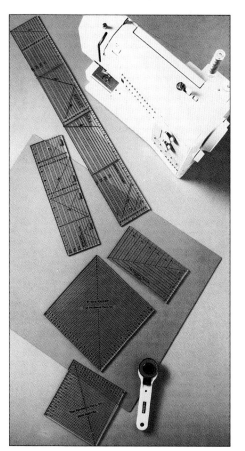

Fabric

FABRIC SELECTION

For best results, select lightweight, closely woven, 100 percent cotton fabrics. Polyester content may make small patchwork pieces difficult to cut and sew accurately.

While 100 percent cotton is ideal, it is not always possible with quilts created from fabric collections of long-standing. Some of my most interesting prints were purchased before I followed the 100 percent rule—they are polyester/cotton blends of uncertain content. I know I shouldn't use them, but the colors and prints are unobtainable today and often serve a unique design purpose in the quilt.

FABRIC LIBRARY

The success of a multi-fabric quilt, which relies on color groups or runs rather than the use of a single print in a certain color, is dependent upon a well-stocked "fabric library." Making multi-fabric quilts has changed my fabric shopping.

I rarely purchase specific fabric for a specific quilt. When I purchase new fabric, it is with the goal of enriching my fabric library. I purchase three to four yards of any fabric that would make a good background fabric. These are mainly lighter fabrics—white, beige, taupe, ecru, pink, lavender, and blue with a white background. I purchase

from one-half to two yards of medium- to dark-toned prints, depending on how much I like the color and design.

Because I want my quilt to look different from other quilts, I rely on a special group of fabrics to give my quilts individuality—decorator fabrics. These are 100 percent cotton fabrics normally used for draperies, slipcovers, and pillows. The larger scale of chintzes and decorator prints creates movement and design interest when combined with other fabrics in a quilt.

I have an assortment of chintzes and decorator fabrics in several color groupings. Although these fabrics are heavier than more traditional quilt fabrics, they are not difficult to handle. Many have a glazed finish, which adds a sheen, reflecting light from the quilt's surface.

To gain the maximum effect from large-scale decorator prints, use them for the largest pieces of your block or in alternate blocks. Paisleys were used effectively in the large triangles in Lost Ships Signature on page 25 while Anvil on page 21 contains decorator fabric resembling a toile de Jouy print in the sashings and borders.

Decorator fabrics may add extra bulk to the seams of your quilt. Consider this when planning the quilting design and avoid close quilting in these areas.

Constant evaluation of your fabric library ensures that you have a variety of colors available in all color groups.

COLOR RECIPE

Working with a color recipe will add variety to your quilt. Select a quilt or block and study its design. Assign a color family to a particular area of the block. An example is shown below.

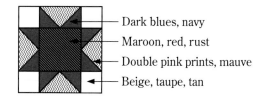

Then, pull a run of colors for each color family, selecting a variety of prints and visual textures from your fabric library. Do not overmatch the colors chosen, but select a range of colors. For instance, if you are pulling a color run of red fabrics, select maroons, deep reds, rusty reds, true reds, and possibly even a warm brown print with red overtones. As you stitch each block, combine different fabrics from the various color families, adhering to your fabric recipe. Try to make blocks with both high and low contrast. The result will be a multi-fabric quilt, where each block is not identical but is unified by the repetition of colors in the color recipe.

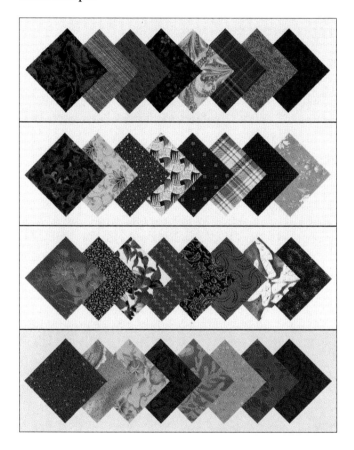

It's fun to make a quilt following a fabric recipe because each resulting block will be different. Feel free to experiment with unusual prints and color arrangements. Push yourself; be adventurous. Go beyond what you consider "safe" fabric and color usage. Break a few rules. Forget about centering large motifs; cabbage roses and other large prints work better when they are cut randomly. Stripes and plaids can be cut randomly, too—even off grain if you wish. Try using the wrong side of some prints to get just the right tone. If you make a mistake in piecing, consider leaving it in to create interest. Most of all, have fun as you try the many options that will make your quilt unique.

SAMPLE BLOCKS

Once you have determined your color recipe and pulled color runs of fabric from your fabric library, it is time to test the recipe by making sample blocks. Since cutting directions on each pattern page are given for the entire quilt, you will need to study the sample block illustration found on each pattern page.

In a multi-fabric quilt, it is necessary to make several sample blocks to determine the effectiveness of the color recipe. Overuse of a color, color integration, contrast, and unity are hard to determine in a single block.

FABRIC PREPARATION

Wash all fabrics first to preshrink, test for colorfastness, and get rid of excess dye. Continue to wash fabric until the rinse water is completely clear. Add a square of white fabric to each washing of the fabric. When this white fabric remains its original color, the fabric is colorfast. A cupful of vinegar in the rinse water may also be used to help set difficult dyes.

Do not use any fabric of which you are uncertain. Many people avoid prewashing their fabric because they prefer to work on "fresh fabric" or because they plan to have the item dry-cleaned. However, colors in the fabric may run if they accidentally get wet, and color dyes are also apt to rub off. Do take time to make sure all of your fabrics are colorfast.

After washing, press fabric and fold into fourths lengthwise. Make straight cuts with the rotary cutter across each end. When using a length of fabric, make straight cuts from one end and bias cuts from the other end. Then, fold the fabric and store it with others of the same color.

Make it a habit to wash and prepare fabrics after they are purchased and before they are placed in the fabric library. Then, your fabric will be ready to sew when you are.

Rotary Cutting

WORKING WITH GRAIN LINES

Yarns are woven together to form fabric, giving it the ability to stretch or remain stable, depending on the grain line you are using. Lengthwise grain runs parallel to the selvage and has very little stretch. Crosswise grain runs from selvage to selvage and has some "give" to it. All other grains are considered bias. True bias is a grain line that runs at a 45° angle to the lengthwise and crosswise grains.

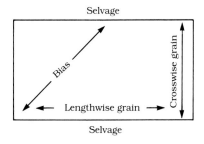

If fabric is badly off grain, pull diagonally as shown to straighten. It is impossible to rotary cut fabrics exactly on the straight grain of fabric since many fabrics are printed off grain. In rotary cutting, straight, even cuts are made as close to the grain as possible. A slight variation from the grain will not alter your project.

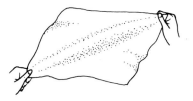

In most cases, the rotary-cutting directions have been written using the following guides for grain-line placement:

1. Strips are cut on the crosswise grain of fabric.
2. Squares and rectangles are cut on the lengthwise and crosswise grain of fabric.
3. Half-square triangles are cut with the short sides on the straight grain and the long side on the bias. Bias strip piecing produces sewn half-square triangles whose grain lines follow this guideline.

4. Quarter-square triangles have the short sides on the bias and the long side on the straight grain. They are generally used along the outside edges of individual blocks or quilts where the long edge will not stretch.
5. When working with striped fabric or directional prints, the direction of the stripe or print takes precedence over the direction of the grain. Handle these pieces carefully since they might not be cut on grain and will therefore be less stable. If these pieces are to be used along the outside edges of the quilt, staystitch ⅛" from the raw edges to avoid stretching.

STRAIGHT CUTS

Cut all pieces with the ¼" seam allowance included. If accurate ¼" seams are sewn by machine, there is no need to mark stitching lines. To cut squares, rectangles, and triangles, you will first need to cut straight strips of fabric.

1. Align the Bias Square® with the fold of fabric and place a cutting guide to the left. When making all cuts, fabric should be placed to your right. (Reverse these techniques if you are left-handed.)

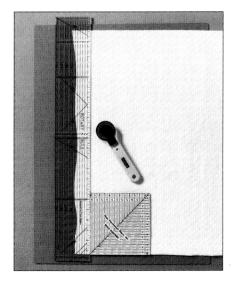

2. Remove the Bias Square and make a rotary cut along right side of ruler. Hold ruler down with left hand, placing smallest finger off the ruler.

This serves as an anchor and keeps ruler from moving. Move hand along ruler as you make the cut, making sure the markings remain accurate. Use firm, even pressure as you rotary cut. Begin rolling the cutter before crossing the folded fabric edge and continue across the fabric. Always roll cutter away from you; never pull cutter toward you.

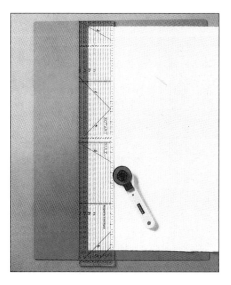

3. Fold fabric lengthwise again so that you will be cutting four layers at a time. (This means shorter cuts.) Open and check the fabric periodically to make sure you are making straight cuts. If fabric strips are not straight, use the Bias Square®, cutting guide, and rotary cutter to straighten the edge again.
4. All fabric is placed to the right and measured from the left straight edge. Rulers or the Bias Square and rulers can be combined to make cuts wider than 3½".

BIAS CUTS

Bias strips for bias squares and binding are cut in the following manner:

1. Align the 45° marking of ruler along the selvage and make a bias cut.
2. Measure width of the strip from cut edge of fabric. Cut along edge of ruler.

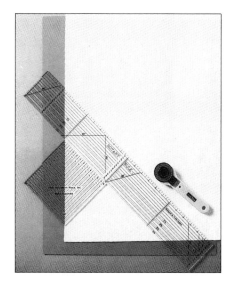

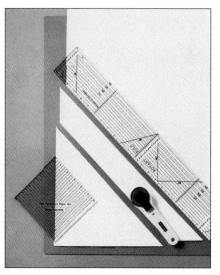

SQUARES AND RECTANGLES

1. First cut fabric into strips the measurement of the square, plus seam allowances.
2. Using the Bias Square®, align top and bottom edge of strip and cut fabric into squares the width of the strip.
3. Rectangles are cut in the same manner, first cutting strips into the shortest measurement of the rectangle.

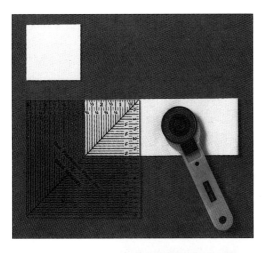

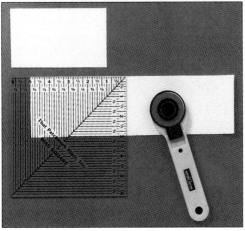

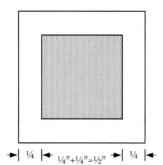

4. To cut a small, odd-sized square or rectangle for which there is no marking on your cutting guide, make an accurate paper template (including ¼" seam allowances). Tape it to the bottom of the Bias Square® and you will have the correct alignment for cutting strips or squares.

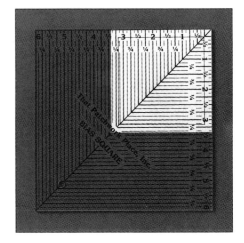

HALF-SQUARE TRIANGLES

Most of the triangles used in these quilts are half-square triangles. These triangles are half of a square with the short sides on the straight grain of fabric and the long side on the bias. To cut these triangles, cut a square and then cut it in half diagonally. Cut the square ⅞" larger than the finished short side of the triangle to allow for seam allowances.

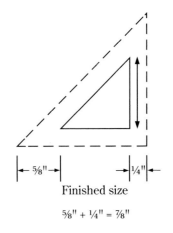

Finished size

⅝" + ¼" = ⅞"

1. Cut a strip the desired finished measurement, plus ⅞".
2. Then, cut strip into squares using the same measurement.

3. Cut a stack of squares diagonally, from corner to corner.

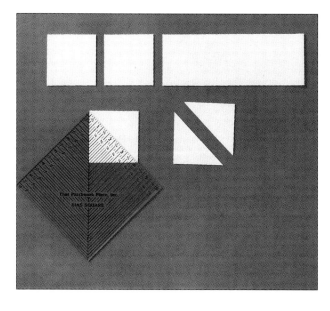

QUARTER-SQUARE TRIANGLES

Triangles whose longest sides are used along the outside edges of blocks and quilts are usually quarter-square triangles. These triangles are cut from squares so their short sides are on the bias and the long side is on the straight of grain. This makes them easier to handle and keeps the outside edges of your quilt from stretching. Cut the square 1¼" larger than the finished long side of the triangle.

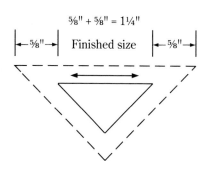

Trimming Points for Easy Matching

The Bias Square® can be used to trim seam-allowance points on half-square triangles. The measurement to use is the finished short side of the triangle plus ½" (¼" seam allowance on each side). The example shown here is a half-square triangle with a finished dimension of 4".

1. To quick-cut this triangle, cut a 4⅞" square of fabric and cut it in half once diagonally.
2. To trim the points for easy matching, set the Bias Square® at the 4½" mark on the fabric triangle as shown. The points of the triangle will extend ⅜". Trim them off with the rotary cutter.

1. Cut a strip the desired finished measurement, plus 1¼".
2. Then, cut strip into squares using the same measurement.
3. Cut a stack of these squares (at least four) diagonally, lining up the ruler from corner to opposite corner. Without moving these pieces, cut in the other direction to create the X cut. Each square will yield four triangles with the long side on grain.

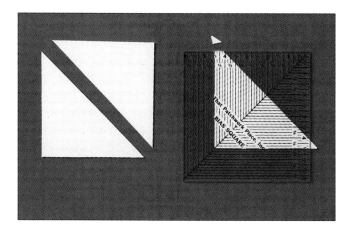

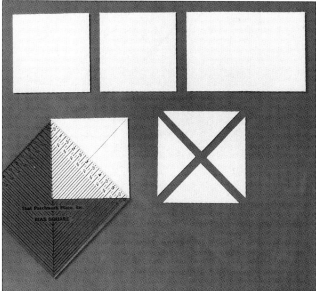

MAKING BIAS SQUARES

Many traditional quilt patterns contain squares made from two contrasting half-square triangles. The short sides of the triangles are on the straight grain of fabric while the long sides are on the bias. These are called bias-square units. Using a bias strip-piecing method, you can easily sew and cut bias squares in many sizes. This technique is especially useful for small bias squares, where pressing after stitching usually distorts the shape (and sometimes burns fingers!).

Basic Technique

1. To make fabric more manageable, cut two half-yard pieces of contrasting fabric and layer with right sides facing up. Both fabric strips will be cut at the same time.
2. Use the 45° marking on the cutting guide and then use a longer ruler to make a bias cut.

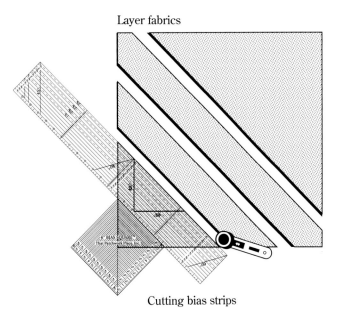

Cutting bias strips

3. In most cases, strips are cut the same width as the bias squares you will be cutting. For example, cut bias strips 2½" wide for 2½" cut bias squares. After piecing, you will have 2" finished bias squares. This is an easy general rule to remember, but specific strip widths are provided with the quilt directions.
4. Sew the strips together on the long bias edge with ¼" seams. Press seams toward the darker fabric. (If cutting bias squares 1¼" or smaller,

you may want to press the seams open to evenly distribute the fabric bulk.)

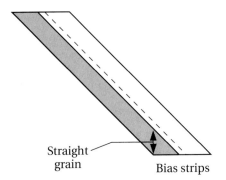

Straight grain

Bias strips

5. Align 45° marking of the Bias Square® with seam line. Cut first two sides of square after measuring distance from cut edge to opposite side of square. Measure and cut third and fourth sides in the same manner.

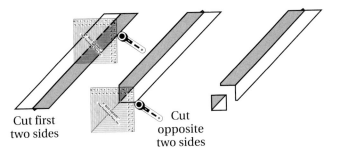

Cut first two sides

Cut opposite two sides

6. Align 45° marking on the Bias Square® with the seam line before cutting the next bias square.

Note: All directions in this book give cut size for bias squares; finished size after stitching will be ½" smaller.

Edge Triangles

When bias squares are cut from long bias strips of fabric, there are leftover triangular pieces along each side. We refer to these pieces as edge triangles, and some of the quilt directions utilize them in constructing the blocks. First, these edge triangles must be resized. Directions are given on page 16 for resizing edge triangles, using the new ScrapSaver™ cutting guide. When the quilt does not make use of the edge triangles, you can save them and resize them for other quilts, using the ScrapSaver™.

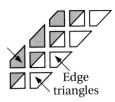

Edge triangles

CUTTING MULTIPLE BIAS SQUARES

To conserve time and fabric, several cutting formats have been devised to produce bias squares. Each format results in different colorations of bias squares and contains variations in the number of strips sewn together. All strips are cut from half-yard lengths of fabric.

A cutting format is illustrated with the cutting directions for each quilt. The size of the bias squares and the number of strips sewn together determine the cut width of the strips. The number of edge triangles needed for each quilt determines the number of strips sewn together. If the cutting format does not provide enough edge triangles for your design, you will find quick-cutting information for additional triangles with the directions.

Cutting Format #1: Bias Squares in Two Colors

1. Follow basic technique on page 12 to prepare strips for bias squares, using the cutting width specified in the quilt directions.
2. Join two, four, five, or six bias strips of fabric together, alternating dark and light strips.

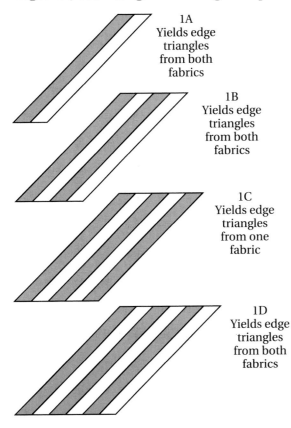

1A
Yields edge triangles from both fabrics

1B
Yields edge triangles from both fabrics

1C
Yields edge triangles from one fabric

1D
Yields edge triangles from both fabrics

3. Begin at lower end of strips and cut the first two sides of the bias squares, aligning 45° marking on the seam line.

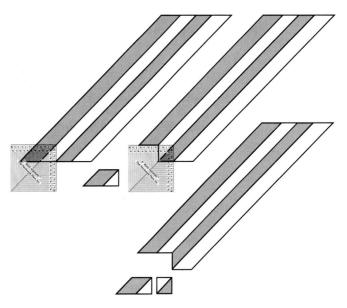

4. Turn cut segments and place Bias Square® on the opposite two sides, accurately aligning the measurements on both sides of the cutting guide and the 45° marking. Cut remaining two sides of bias squares.

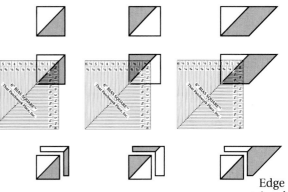

Edge triangle

5. Cut bias squares from the next row, working up the strip.
6. Continue cutting bias squares, until you have used all of the fabric.
7. Resize any edge triangles needed for design, using the ScrapSaver™ cutting guide (page 16).

Cutting Format #2: Bias Squares of a Consistent Background Color

If you are using a consistent background color in your bias squares, such as muslin with a variety of other prints, use the following technique:

1. Follow basic technique on page 12 to prepare strips for bias squares, using the cutting width specified in the pattern.
2. Join three, four, five, or six bias strips of fabric together, alternating the chosen background fabric with the others.

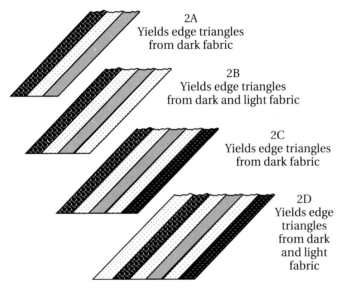

2A
Yields edge triangles
from dark fabric

2B
Yields edge triangles
from dark and light fabric

2C
Yields edge triangles
from dark fabric

2D
Yields edge
triangles
from dark
and light
fabric

3. Follow steps 3–7 of Cutting Format #1 to cut bias squares.

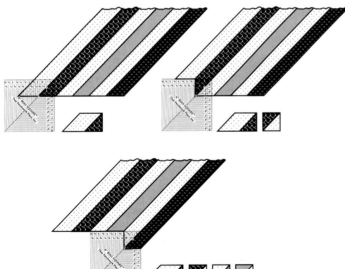

Note: You can also make a dark variation, using black for a background color.

Cutting Format #3: Multicolor Bias Squares

1. Follow basic technique on page 12 to prepare strips for bias squares, using the cutting width specified in the pattern.
2. Join six strips of different fabrics together.

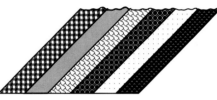

Cutting format #3

3. Follow steps 3–7 of Cutting Format #1 to cut bias squares.

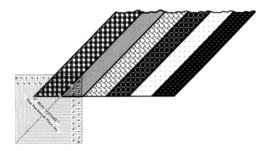

UTILIZING SHORTER STRIPS

When sewing bias strips together, you can also utilize the shorter strips that are cut from the corners of the fabric. If you are using fat quarters in your projects, you will have many of these short strips. They may be used to "square off" the sides of the longer strips cut from half-yard lengths or in a separate piecing configuration of their own. Just remember to alternate dark and light strips.

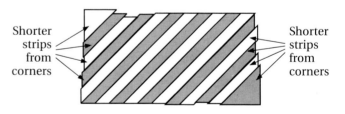

Shorter strips from corners

Shorter strips from corners

ROTARY CUTTING A MULTI-FABRIC QUILT FROM YARDAGE

A Template-Free™ rotary-cutting approach can be used for most quilts. With a little planning, it is possible to rotary cut a multi-fabric quilt and not have too many repetitions of fabric combinations.

For each quilt in this book, a "Materials" list specifies the total amount of fabric needed for a particular color group. Pull appropriate amounts of differing fabrics within that color group from your fabric library. If three yards of dark blue fabrics are required, pull half-yard pieces of at least six different blue prints. It sometimes helps to vary the amount of each print used within a color grouping. Some prints are too dominant and eye-catching to be used frequently. Since they interrupt the unity of the quilt, use them in smaller amounts. Use larger amounts of smaller, more restful prints, which help the design flow from one area of the quilt to another.

When a quilt requires bias squares, that is the first cutting specification given. From half-yard pieces of fabric, cut bias strips of fabric. If the bias squares are to be constructed of light blue and dark blue fabric, cut light blue and dark blue bias strips from the six different blue prints.

Use the same procedure when cutting larger squares and triangles. If you need thirty-five assorted dark squares, 6⅞" x 6⅞", cut several from each fabric. For example, if seven different dark fabrics are used, cut five from each dark fabric. Using the rotary cutter will save you time since you won't need to make templates. You merely cut a 6⅞"-wide strip from each piece of fabric. Then, stack the strips and make 6⅞"-wide cuts across each strip to make the squares. If cutting triangles from these squares, make the diagonal cut or cuts before moving the stack of squares. It is easiest to work with a small mat, turning it to get the proper cutting angle for diagonal cuts. Moving the squares may cause fabric to shift, creating inaccurate cuts.

As you use these segments in your blocks, be sure to select different bias-square color combinations as well as triangles and squares of different colors. Vary the emphasis within each block. One block may blend with restful prints and low-contrast colors while another offers high contrast with a variety of stripes and polka dots.

When you lay out the blocks for your quilt top, also vary the placement of strong prints and high- and low-contrast blocks. By scattering these

elements evenly through your quilt top, you will keep the eye moving, causing one to look at the quilt longer. Or, you may want to group all the low-contrast or soft colors in one area of the quilt, creating a flow into stronger contrast or brighter color. Each step of the quilt construction will give you the opportunity to make new design choices and add more individuality.

ROTARY CUTTING A MULTI-FABRIC QUILT FROM SCRAPS

Many blocks and quilts contain units made from half-square triangles. Using the ScrapSaver™, you can quickly cut half-square triangles in an assortment of useful sizes from your odd-shaped scraps and from the edge triangles that result when cutting bias squares.

To quick-cut half-square triangles, we typically add ⅞" to the desired finished size of a short side of the triangle, cut a square to that measurement, and divide the square on the diagonal. This technique allows for ¼" seam allowances and yields two half-square triangles, with the short sides on the straight grain of the fabric and the long side on the bias.

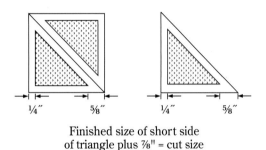

Finished size of short side
of triangle plus ⅞" = cut size

With the ScrapSaver™ tool, half-square triangles can be quick-cut individually, without first cutting a square. The tool is marked for cutting 1⅞", 2⅜", 2⅞", 3⅜", and 3⅞" half-square triangles; with ¼" seams, the short sides will finish to 1", 1½", 2", 2½", and 3".

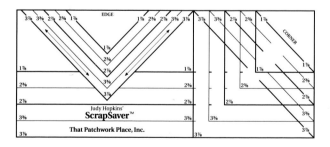

To use the Scrapsaver™, you will need a rotary cutter and a cutting mat. A small cutting mat is very useful as you can rotate the mat to get the proper cutting angle without disturbing the fabric. Press your scraps before you begin, then cut as described in the following paragraphs. Several scraps can be stacked for cutting. Place the largest piece on the bottom and the smallest piece on top, aligning any square corners or true bias edges.

Remember:
For 1" (finished) triangles, use the 1⅞" lines.
For 1½" (finished) triangles, use the 2⅜" lines.
For 2" (finished) triangles, use the 2⅞" lines.
For 2½" (finished) triangles, use the 3⅜" lines.
For 3" (finished) triangles, use the 3⅞" lines.

For scraps with square corners (common with bias-square edge triangles):
Align the corner of the scrap with the proper edge-triangle lines of the ScrapSaver™ and cut along straight edge to remove excess fabric.

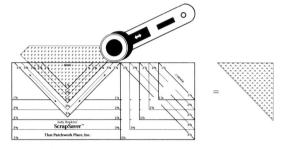

For scraps with true bias edges:
Align the bias edge of the scrap with the proper corner-triangle line of the ScrapSaver™ and cut along two straight edges to remove excess fabric.

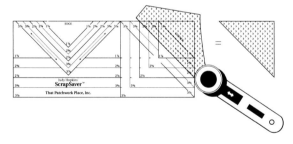

For scraps with no square corners or true bias edges:
Lay the corner triangle of the ScrapSaver™ over the scrap, aligning the ruler with the grain of the fabric and making sure that the corner-triangle line for the size you wish to cut does not extend beyond the fabric. Cut along the two straight edges, making a square corner.

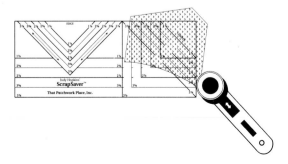

Align the square corner with the proper edge-triangle lines and cut along the straight edge to remove the excess fabric.

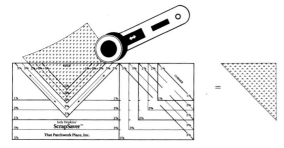

For larger scraps:

Lay the corner square of the ScrapSaver™ over the scrap, aligning the ruler with the grain of the fabric and making sure that the corner-square lines for the size you wish to cut do not extend beyond the fabric. Cut along the two straight edges, making a square corner.

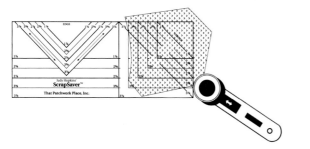

Rotate the cutting mat or turn the cut piece of fabric, align the corner you just cut with the proper corner-square lines, and cut along the two straight edges again to make a square.

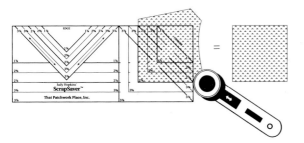

Align a corner of the square with the proper edge-triangle lines and cut along the straight edge to divide the square into two triangles.

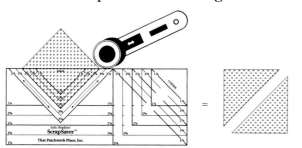

For large rectangular scraps:

Align a long edge of the ScrapSaver™ with the grain of the fabric and cut along the ruler to remove the uneven edge of the scrap.

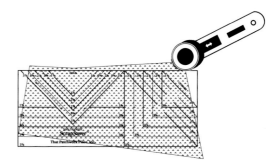

Rotate the cutting mat or turn the cut piece of fabric and align the proper long line with the straight cut you just made, letting the scrap extend just beyond the top of the ruler; cut along the two straight edges to make a square corner.

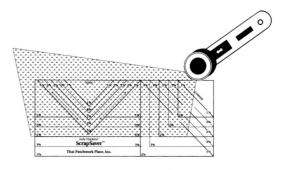

Align a square corner with the proper corner-square lines and cut along the straight edge to complete the square.

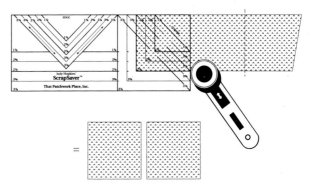

Repeat until you have cut as many squares as possible from the strip. Divide the squares, using the proper edge-triangle lines as shown above.

Machine Piecing

A well-maintained, straight-stitch sewing machine is adequate for all quiltmaking operations. Use sewing machine needles sized for cotton fabrics (size 70/10 or 80/12) and change them frequently; dull or bent needles can snag and distort your fabric and cause skipped stitches. Set stitch length at 10–12 stitches per inch; make sure the top and bobbin tensions are properly adjusted. Judy uses a medium greenish-gray thread for piecing all but the lightest and darkest fabrics—the color you get when you mix all the Easter egg dyes together. If an even-feed ("walking") foot is available for your machine, it is worth buying one. You will find it invaluable for sewing on bindings and for machine quilting.

Learn to sew a precise ¼" seam. Find the ¼" seam allowance on your machine by placing an accurate template under the presser foot and lowering the needle onto the seam line; mark the seam allowance by placing a piece of masking tape or moleskin at the edge of the template.

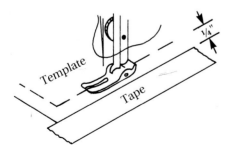

You can save time and thread by chain piecing. Place the pieces that are to be joined right sides together; pin as necessary. Stitch the seam, but do not lift the presser foot or cut the threads; just feed in the next set of pieces as close as possible to the last set. Sew as many seams as you can; clip the threads between the pieces.

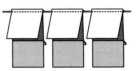

Judy presses seams open to make it easier to hand stitch the allover quilting patterns she commonly uses for her quilts. However, the traditional quilters' rule is to press seams to one side, toward the darker fabric when possible. Side-pressed seams are stronger, and it is easier for most people to make corners meet properly when they can match opposing seams.

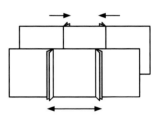

Keep your iron and ironing board close to the sewing machine. Frequent, gentle steam pressing is important; be careful not to distort your pieces with heavy-handed ironing. An iron with both spray and shot-of-stem features is very helpful.

Quilt Patterns

This section contains complete instructions for forty rotary-cut quilts. All of the patterns are written for rotary cutting; no templates are provided. Read the complete cutting and piecing directions for the quilt you are going to make before you begin. The patterns are graded with symbols as to difficulty, so match the pattern to your skill level.

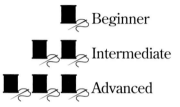

The "Materials" section of each pattern includes fabric and color suggestions. Fabric requirements are based on 44"-wide fabric that has 42 useable inches. If your fabric is not at least 42" wide, you may need to purchase more. The amounts given are adequate for the project; there will be little or no leftover fabric.

Cutting instructions are geared for rotary cutting. Quick-cutting and strip-piecing techniques sometimes yield more pieces than are actually needed to make a particular block or quilt; don't worry if you have a few more pieces than you need. All measurements for block pieces include ¼" seam allowances. *Do not add seam allowances to the dimensions given in the cutting section.*

Cutting specifications for triangles indicate the size of the square from which the triangles will be cut. Directions for half-square triangles instruct you to "cut diagonally"; for quarter-square triangles, you are told to "cut twice diagonally." If you need a refresher, see the section that begins on page 8.

Use the photos and drawings that accompany the patterns as a reference while assembling your quilt. If you need help setting blocks on point, see the section that begins on page 104.

Borders with straight-cut corners rather than mitered corners are used except where otherwise noted. Border strips are cut along the crosswise grain and seamed where extra length is needed; purchase additional fabric if you want to cut borders along the lengthwise grain. Border pieces are cut extra long, then trimmed to fit when the actual dimensions of the center section of the quilt are known. (See the "Borders" section beginning on page 107.) Bindings are narrow, double-fold, made from straight or bias strips. (See the "Bindings" section, starting on page 112, if you need basic information on applying bindings.) Backings are pieced horizontally when seaming is necessary. (See the Backings and Batting section on page 109.)

In several of the patterns, the instructions result in a quilt that differs slightly from the quilt in the photograph; watch for the special notations that describe these differences. Though all the patterns have been written for strip piecing or bias squares, you will see that some of the photographed quilts have been made with individually cut pieces. The fabric requirements given should accommodate either method, but you will have to alter the cutting instructions if you prefer a more traditional approach.

General instructions for finishing your quilt begin on page 103.

Anvil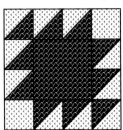

Anvil
8" block

Dimensions: 62" x 83"

35 blocks, 8", set 5 across and 7 down with 2½"-wide sashing; 6"-wide border.

Materials: 44"-wide fabric

3 yds. assorted dark prints in navy, purple, burgundy, and black for anvil
3 yds. assorted light prints for background
2⅛ yds. figured print for sashing and borders
4 yds. fabric for backing
⅝ yd. fabric for 296" of binding
Batting and thread to finish

Cutting: All measurements include ¼" seams.

From the dark and light assorted prints:
Using Cutting Format #2B (page 14), cut and piece 18 sets of 2½"-wide bias strips to make 350 bias squares. Each set of strips will yield 21 bias squares, 2½" x 2½". You will need 10 matching bias squares for each Anvil block. Edge triangles are not used in this quilt.

From the remainder of the assorted light prints:
Cut 70 squares, 2½" x 2½", with 2 to match the light print of each Anvil block.

From the remainder of the assorted dark prints:
Cut 35 squares, 4½" x 4½", with 1 to match the dark print used in each Anvil block.

From the figured print (cut lengthwise):
Cut 2 borders, 6½" x 71½", for sides.
Cut 2 borders, 6½" x 62", for top and bottom.
Cut 28 sashing pieces, 3" x 8½".
Cut 6 sashing strips, 3" x 50½".

DIRECTIONS

1. Piece 35 Anvil blocks as shown.

make 2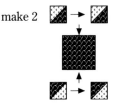

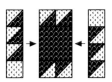

make 2

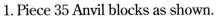

2. Piece 7 rows, using 5 blocks and 4 sashing pieces.
3. Assemble rows with a sashing strip between them.
4. Add side borders, then top and bottom borders to quilt top.
5. Layer with batting and backing; quilt or tie.

Quilting Suggestion: Use an old-fashioned design like hanging diamonds to quilt a diagonal grid across the quilt top and borders.

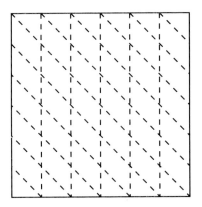

6. Bind with straight or bias strips of fabric.

Anvil by Nancy J. Martin, 1991, Woodinville, Washington, 62" x 83". Inspired by a utility quilt made in Pennsylvania, the toile de Juoy fabric used in the borders and sashing serves as a frame for contemporary fabrics that recall those printed in the late 1800s. Quilted by Freda Smith. (Collection of That Patchwork Place, Inc.)

Kansas Troubles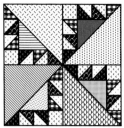

Kansas Troubles
16" block

Dimensions: 74" x 74"

16 blocks, 16", set 4 across and 4 down; 5"-wide border.

Materials: 44"-wide fabric

3 yds. assorted dark blue prints for bias squares
3 yds. assorted light-background prints for bias squares and large triangles
¾ yd. assorted medium blue prints for small triangles
2½ yds. medium blue solid for border
4¼ yds. fabric for backing
⅝ yd. fabric for 300" of binding
Batting and thread to finish

Cutting: All measurements include ¼" seams.

From dark blue and light-background prints:
Using Cutting Format #2C (page 14), cut 10 sets of 2½"-wide bias strips to make 256 bias squares. Each set of strips will yield 28 bias squares, 2½" x 2½". Using the 2⅞" marking on the ScrapSaver™ (page 16), resize edge triangles from dark fabrics. You will need 128 dark triangles or 8 for each block. If additional half-square triangles are needed, cut a 2⅞" square diagonally.

From the medium blue prints:
Cut 32 squares, 4⅞" x 4⅞". Cut diagonally into 64 triangles.

From the remainder of the light-background prints:
Cut 32 squares, 8⅞" x 8⅞". Cut diagonally into 64 triangles.

From the medium blue solid (cut lengthwise):
Cut 2 borders, 5½" x 64½", for sides.
Cut 2 borders, 5½" x 74", for top and bottom.

Directions

1. Piece 16 Kansas Troubles blocks as shown.

Make 4:

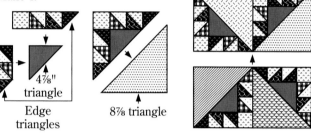

Edge triangles   4⅞" triangle   8⅞ triangle

2. Join blocks together in 4 rows of 4 blocks each.
3. Join rows into quilt top.
4. Add side borders, then top and bottom borders to quilt top.
5. Layer with batting and backing; quilt or tie.

Quilting Suggestion: Create an old-fashioned sampler of quilt designs by dividing the quilt into several areas of unequal size. Quilt a different overall pattern (which does not outline the block design) on each area. Suggested patterns are a straight-line grid, Clamshells, or Baptist Fan.

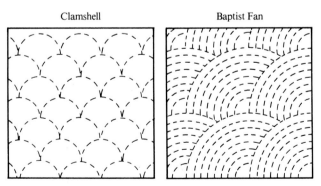

Clamshell   Baptist Fan

6. Bind with straight or bias strips of fabric.

Kansas Troubles by Nancy J. Martin, 1991, Woodinville, Washington, 74" x 74". An assortment of randomly placed blue fabrics gives a soft, pleasing look to this angular design. Various quilting designs create overall patterns on different areas of the quilt, without outlining the block design. Quilted by Sue von Jentzen. (Collection of That Patchwork Place, Inc.)

Lost Ships Signature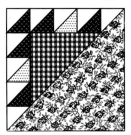

Lost Ships Signature
10" block

Dimensions: 60" x 84"

24 blocks, 10", set 4 across and 6 down with 2"-wide sashing; 5"-wide border.

Materials: 44"-wide fabric

3 yds. muslin or light-background prints for blocks
2½ yds. assorted prints for small triangles and bias squares
2½ yds. paisley or large print for large triangles
1½ yds. green print for sashing
1¼ yds. print for borders (cut crosswise)
3½ yds. fabric for backing
⅝ yd. fabric for 288" of binding
Batting and thread to finish

Cutting: All measurements include ¼" seams.

From the muslin or light-background prints and the assorted prints:

Using Cutting Format #2D (page 14), cut and piece 6 sets of 2½"-wide bias strips to make 203 bias squares. Each set of strips will yield 35 bias squares, 2½" x 2½".You will need 7 matching bias squares for each Lost Ships block. Save extra bias squares for sashing. Using the 2⅞" marking on the ScrapSaver™ (page 16), resize edge triangles from light fabrics. You will need 48 light triangles or 2 for each block. Dark edge triangles are not used in this quilt. If additional half-square triangles are needed, cut a 2⅞" square diagonally.

From the remainder of the assorted prints:

Cut 12 squares, 6⅞" x 6⅞". Cut diagonally to make 24 small triangles.

From the paisley or large print:

Cut 12 squares, 10⅞" x 10⅞". Cut diagonally to make 24 large triangles.

From the green print:

Cut 58 strips, 2½" x 10½", for sashing.

From the border print:

Cut 8 strips, 5½" x 44", for borders.

DIRECTIONS

1. Piece 24 Lost Ships blocks as shown.

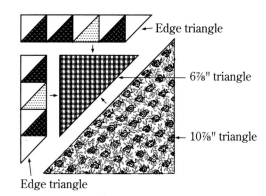

Edge triangle
6⅞" triangle
10⅞" triangle
Edge triangle

2. Piece 6 rows, using 4 blocks and 5 sashing pieces.
3. Assemble 7 rows of sashing, using 4 sashing pieces and 5 bias squares for each row as shown in the photo.
4. Assemble rows of blocks with rows of sashing between them to form quilt top.
5. Seam border strips together to make two 5½" x 74½" strips for sides of quilt top and two 5½" x 60" strips for top and bottom.
6. Stitch side borders to quilt top, then add borders to top and bottom.
7. Layer with batting and backing; quilt or tie.

Quilting Suggestion: Quilt a Clamshell design (page 22) inside the large triangles. Quilt diagonal lines through the remainder of the block. Create a "picture frame" border, using diagonal lines that slant in a different direction on each side of the border.

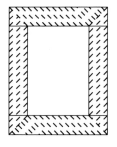

8. Bind with straight or bias strips of fabric.

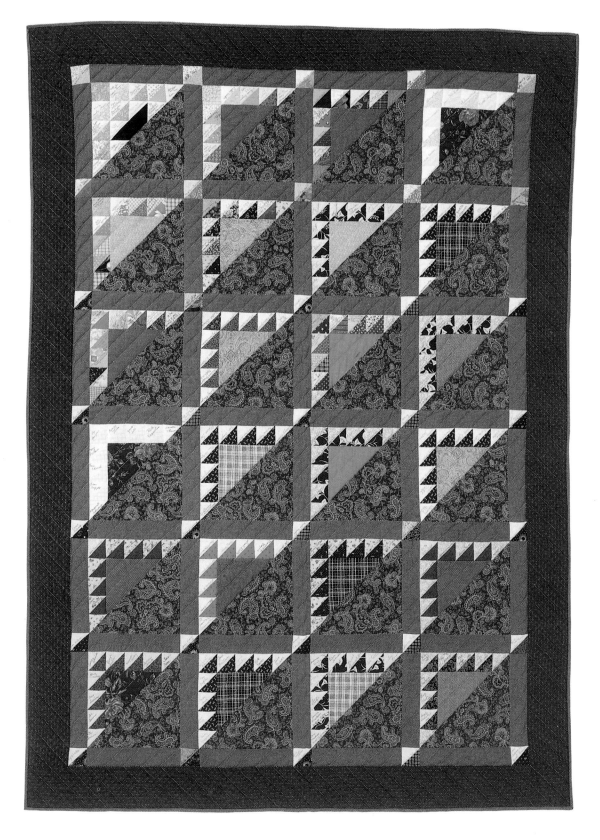

Lost Ships Signature Quilt by Nancy J. Martin, 1990, Woodinville, Washington, 60" x 84".
The large-scale paisley print and soft green lattices help to unify the wide range of colors used
in the bias squares, many donated by Nancy's students. Each square in this wonderful
memory quilt contains a signature of quilting friends and students, collected from both
home and abroad. Quilted by Freda Smith.

Fruit Basket

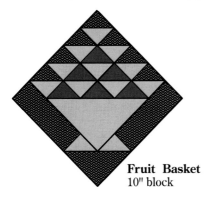

Fruit Basket
10" block

Dimensions: 64½" x 64½"

9 blocks, 10", diagonally set 3 across and 3 down with unpieced alternate blocks; 1"-wide inner border; 10"-wide outer border with corner squares.

Materials: 44"-wide fabric

½ yd. each of 9 brightly colored solids for baskets
1½ yds. dark print for background, alternate
   blocks, and corner squares
¼ yd. brightly colored print for inner border
1½ yds. brightly colored print for outer border
3¾ yds. fabric for backing
½ yd. fabric for 264" of binding
Batting and thread to finish

Cutting: All measurements include ¼" seams.

From the dark print and brightly colored solids:
   Using Cutting Format #2A (page 14), cut and piece 5 sets of 2½"-wide strips to make 63 bias squares. Each set of strips will yield 14 bias squares, 2½" x 2½".Using the 2⅞" marking on the ScrapSaver™ (page 16), resize edge triangles from brightly colored solids. You will need 18, with 2 to match the color of each basket base. If additional half-square triangles are needed, cut a 2⅞" square diagonally.

From the remainder of the brightly colored solids:
   Cut 9 triangles for baskets, each 6⅞", along the straight grain.

Using Cutting Format #3 (page 14), cut and piece 2 sets of 2½"-wide bias strips to make 27 bias squares. Each set of strips will yield 35 bias squares, 2½" x 2½". Using the 2⅞" marking on the ScrapSaver™ (page 16), resize edge triangles from brightly colored solids. You will need 27, 3 to use in top of each Basket block. If additional half-square triangles are needed, cut a 2⅞" square diagonally.

From the remainder of the dark print:
   Cut 5 squares, 4⅞" x 4⅞". Cut diagonally for 9 triangles.
   Cut 18 rectangles, 2½" x 6½".
   Cut 8 squares, 10½" x 10½", for alternate blocks and corner squares.
   Cut 2 squares, 15½" x 15½", for set pieces to be used along sides. Cut twice diagonally to yield 8 triangles.
   Cut 2 squares, 8" x 8", for corner set pieces. Cut diagonally for 4 triangles.

From the brightly colored print for inner border:
   Cut 4 strips, 1½" x 43".

From the brightly colored print for outer border:
   Cut 4 strips, 10½" x 45".

From any brightly colored fabric:
   Cut 4 small corner squares, 1½" x 1½".

DIRECTIONS

1. Piece 9 Fruit Basket blocks as shown. Mix and match the bias squares inside the basket shape.

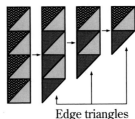

Edge triangles

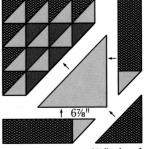

6⅞"

4⅞" triangle

Note: Not all solid-colored fabrics in the handle match the basket. Resize edge triangles for the basket base to match basket color.

2. Join Fruit Basket blocks into diagonal rows with alternate blocks, side, and corner set pieces.
3. Join rows together to form the quilt top.
4. Stitch 2 inner borders to opposite sides of quilt top. Add a small corner square to each end of the other inner borders. Stitch inner borders (with corner squares attached) to remaining sides of quilt top.
5. Stitch 2 outer borders to opposite sides of quilt top. Add large corner squares to each end of the other 2 outer borders. Stitch outer borders (with corner squares attached) to remaining sides of quilt top.
6. Layer with batting and backing; quilt or tie.

Quilting Suggestion: Use dark thread to outline each basket shape. Add curvy lines inside basket base. Repeat an angular design, such as Fandango (page 123) or Stock Market (page 121), in border. In the quilt shown in the photo, the angular lines contrast nicely with the curvy printed shapes on the background fabric.

7. Bind with straight or bias strips of fabric.

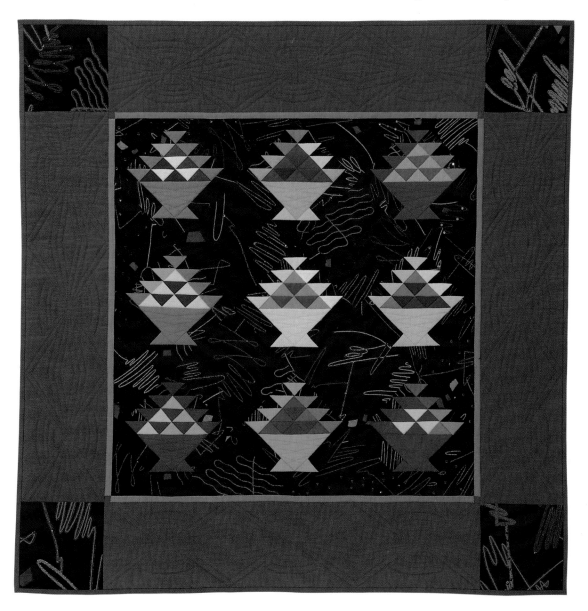

Celebration by Joyce Stewart, 1988, Rexberg, Idaho, 64½ x 64½". Brightly colored baskets are set against the wrong side of an electrifying dark print. The right side of this same print was used for the corner squares.

Crown of Thorns

Crown of Thorns
10" block

Dimensions: 68" x 81"

30 blocks, 10", set 5 across and 6 down with 3"-wide sashing; 3"-wide outer border.

Materials: 44"-wide fabric

4 yds. assorted light-background prints for blocks
4 yds. assorted dark prints in brown, navy, black, and purple for blocks
2½ yds. black print for sashing and borders
4¾ yds. fabric for backing
⅝ yd. fabric for 302" of binding
Batting and thread to finish

Cutting: All measurements include ¼" seams.

From the assorted light-background and dark prints:
Using Cutting Format #2D (page 14), cut and piece 14 sets of 2½"-wide bias strips to make a total of 480 bias squares. Each set of strips will yield 35 bias squares, 2½" x 2½". Edge triangles are not used in this quilt.

From the remainder of the light-background prints:
Cut 150 squares, 2½" x 2½", matching 5 squares to the background fabric in each block.

From the remainder of the dark prints:
Cut 120 squares, 2½" x 2½", matching 4 squares to the dark print in each block.

From the black print for sashing (cut lengthwise):
Cut 24 sashing pieces, 3½" x 10½".
Cut 7 sashing strips, 3½" x 62½".
Cut 2 outer borders, 3½" x 81", for sides.

DIRECTIONS

1. Piece 30 Crown of Thorns blocks.

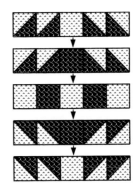

2. Join 5 blocks in a row with 4 sashing pieces. Make 6 rows.
3. Join rows together with sashing strips and add a sashing strip above and below the top and bottom rows.
4. Add remaining outer borders to sides.
5. Layer with batting and backing; quilt or tie.

   Quilting Suggestion: Quilt ¼" inside the seam line on all dark prints.

6. Bind with straight or bias strips of fabric.

Note: This antique quilt has a "whisker cloth" stitched along the top edge, covering a portion of the blocks. The purpose of the whisker cloth was to protect the quilt from the abrasiveness of men's beards.

Crown of Thorns by Ellen Vesper Gordon, c. 1900, South Dakota, 68" x 81". Leona Harleman taught the women of the Yakima Indian Mission to quilt, using this top pieced by her grandmother. A whisker cloth covers the top of the quilt to protect it from the abrasiveness of a man's beard. (Photo by Skip Howard)

Double T

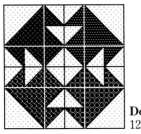

Double T
12" block

Dimensions: 77" x 84"

42 blocks, 12", set 6 across and 7 down; 2½"-wide side borders.

Materials: 44"-wide fabric

4½ yds. pink print for background and side
    borders
4 yds. assorted dark prints in brown, navy, red,
    purple, and black for blocks
4½ yds. fabric for backing
⅝ yd. fabric for 330" of binding
Batting and thread to finish

Note: The antique quilt in the photo was made using the template method and several striped fabrics. It is best to avoid striped fabrics for the bias squares, since careful cutting and matching of the stripes is required.

Cutting: All measurements include ¼" seams.

From the pink print and assorted dark prints:

Using Cutting Format #2C (page 14), cut and piece 11 sets of 4½"-wide bias strips to make 168 bias squares. Each set of strips will yield 16 bias squares, 4½" x 4½". Edge triangles are not used in this quilt.

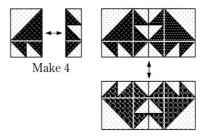

Using Cutting Format #2D (page 14), cut and piece 24 sets of 2½"-wide bias strips to make 840 bias squares. Each set of strips will yield 35 bias squares, 2½" x 2½".

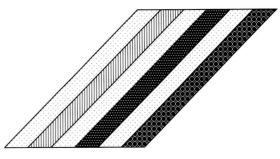

From the remainder of the pink print:
Cut 2 strips, 3" x 84", for side borders.

DIRECTIONS

1. Piece 42 Double T blocks as shown. Use matching bias squares in both sizes to form the shape of the letter "T." A background and 4 different fabrics are used in each block.

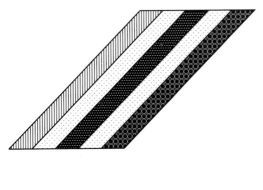

Make 4

2. Join 6 blocks into a row. Make 7 rows.
3. Assemble rows into a quilt top and add borders to each side.
4. Layer with batting and backing; quilt or tie.

Quilting Suggestion: Quilt horizontal and vertical lines across the quilt top. Add diagonal lines to intersect each "T."

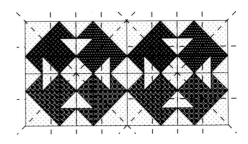

5. Bind with straight or bias strips of fabric.

Double T, maker unknown, c. 1900, Pennsylvania, 77" x 84". Scraps of brown, navy, red, and tan fabrics form the "T" units of each block. The double-pink print used in the background calms the myriad of colors and prints. (Collection of Nancy J. Martin)

Spools

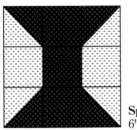

Spools
6" block

Dimensions: 66" x 78"

143 blocks, 6", set 11 across and 13 down; no border.

Materials: 44"-wide fabric

4 yds. assorted light-background prints for blocks
4 yds. assorted dark prints in navy, brown, blue, and black for blocks
4 yds. fabric for backing
⅝ yd. fabric for 300" of binding
Batting and thread to finish

Cutting: All measurements include ¼" seams.

From the light-background and dark prints:
    Using Cutting Format #2C (page 14), cut and piece 21 sets of 2½"-wide bias strips to make 572 bias squares. Each set of strips will yield 28 bias squares, 2½" x 2½". You will need 4 matching bias squares for each block. Edge triangles are not used in this quilt.

From the remainder of the assorted dark prints:
    Cut 143 rectangles, 2½" x 6½".

From the remainder of the light-background prints:
    Cut 286 squares, 2½" x 2½".

DIRECTIONS

1. Piece 143 Spool blocks as shown.

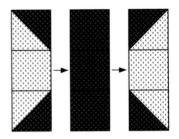

2. Join 11 blocks into a row, alternating the spool from a vertical to a horizontal position across the row. Make 13 rows.
3. Assemble rows into a quilt top.
4. Layer with batting and backing; quilt or tie.

    Quilting Suggestion: Quilt ¼" inside each shape.

5. Bind with straight or bias strips of fabric.

Spools, maker unknown, c. 1900, New York, 66" x 78". The spool pattern is a perennial favorite of quiltmakers. This spirited version combines plaids, homespuns, and shirtings with the dark calico prints of the period. (Collection of Nancy J. Martin)

English Ivy

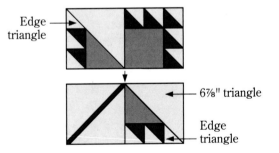

English Ivy
12" block

Dimensions: 84" x 101"

20 blocks, 12", set diagonally with alternate plain blocks; 8"-wide borders.

Materials: 44"-wide fabric

1½ yds. pink fabric for background
1¼ yds. solid-colored burgundy fabric for ivy tips and stems
1¼ yds. rose fabric for ivy
3½ yds. burgundy print for alternate blocks, set pieces, and outer borders
5¾ yds. fabric for backing
¾ yd. fabric for 380" of binding
Batting and thread to finish

Cutting: All measurements include ¼" seams.

From pink and solid-colored burgundy fabric:

Using Cutting Format #1C (page 13), and placing pink strips on the outside edges, cut and piece 7 sets of 2½"-wide bias strips to make 180 bias squares. Each set of strips will yield 28 bias squares, 2½" x 2½". Using the 2⅞" marking on the ScrapSaver™ (page 16), resize edge triangles from pink fabric. If additional half-square triangles are needed, cut a 2⅞" square diagonally.

From the rose fabric:

Cut 20 squares, 4⅞" x 4⅞". Cut diagonally for 40 triangles.
Cut 20 squares, 4½" x 4½".

From the remainder of the pink fabric:

Cut 20 squares, 6⅞" x 6⅞". Cut diagonally for 40 triangles.
Cut 20 squares, 6½" x 6½".

From the remainder of the solid-colored burgundy fabric:

Cut 20 bias strips, 1½" x 9", for stems.

From the burgundy print:

Cut side borders, 8½" x 85", on lengthwise grain.
Cut borders for top and bottom, 8½" x 84", on lengthwise grain.
Cut 12 squares, 12½" x 12½", for alternate blocks.
Cut 4 squares, 18¼" x 18¼". Cut twice diagonally for 14 triangles for side set pieces. (You will have 2 extra triangles to discard or set aside.)
Cut 2 squares, 9⅜" x 9⅜". Cut diagonally into 4 triangles for corner set pieces.

DIRECTIONS

1. Appliqué ivy stems by stitching burgundy bias strip to pink background square.

Fold a 9" x 1¼" strip of bias in thirds; baste.

Applique diagonally from corner to corner on background square.

2. Piece 20 English Ivy blocks as shown.

Edge triangle

6⅞" triangle

Edge triangle

3. Join English Ivy blocks into diagonal rows with alternate blocks, side, and corner set pieces.
4. Join rows together to form the quilt top.
5. Stitch side borders to quilt top, then add borders to top and bottom.
6. Layer with batting and backing; quilt or tie.

Quilting Suggestion: Quilt portions of the Grape Ivy pattern (page 125) in the pink background. Quilt a 12" flower design in the alternate blocks to soften the angular lines.

7. Bind with straight or bias strips of fabric.

English Ivy by Joyce Peaden, 1986, Prosser, Washington, 84" x 101". This traditional block is set in a dark-print background to mimic some of the quilts made in the late 1800s. Quilted by Buena Heights Quilters. (Photo by Skip Howard)

Rosebud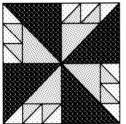

Rosebud
9" block

Dimensions: 60" x 73"

20 blocks, 9", set diagonally with alternate plain blocks; 4½"-wide borders.

Materials: 44"-wide fabric

3¾ yds. light-background print for blocks
1¼ yds. assorted rose and pink prints for blocks
1 yd. assorted green prints for large triangles
3½ yds. fabric for backing
½ yd. fabric for 266" of binding
Batting and thread to finish

Cutting: All measurements include ¼" seams.

From the light-background and rose and pink prints:

Using Cutting Format #2C (page 14), cut and piece 5 sets of 2"-wide bias strips to make 160 bias squares. Each set of strips will yield 36 bias squares, 2" x 2". Using the 2⅜" marking on the ScrapSaver™ (page 16), resize edge triangles from light print. You will need 80 light triangles or 4 for each block. If additional half-square triangles are needed, cut a 2⅜" square diagonally.

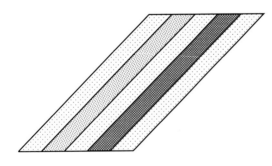

From the remainder of the light-background print:

Cut 12 squares, 9½" x 9½", for alternate blocks.
Cut 4 squares, 14" x 14". Cut twice diagonally into 14 triangles for side set pieces.
Cut 2 squares, 7¼" x 7¼". Cut diagonally into 4 triangles for corner set pieces.
Cut 8 strips, 5" x 44", for borders.

From the remainder of the rose and pink prints:

Cut 40 squares, 3⅞" x 3⅞". Cut diagonally into 80 triangles.

From the green prints:

Cut 40 squares, 5⅜" x 5⅜". Cut diagonally into 80 triangles.

Directions

1. Piece 20 Rosebud blocks as shown.

Edge triangle →

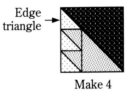

Make 4

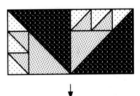

2. Join Rosebud blocks into diagonal rows with alternate blocks, side, and corner set pieces.
3. Join rows together to form the quilt top.
4. Seam border strips together to make two 5" x 64¼" strips for each side of quilt top and two 5" x 60" strips for top and bottom.
5. Stitch side borders to quilt top, then add borders to top and bottom.
6. Layer with batting and backing; quilt or tie.

   Quilting Suggestion: Use an allover pattern, such as Filigree (page 127).

7. Bind with straight or bias strips of fabric.

Kristy's Quilt by Alice Graves, 1991, Girdwood, Alaska, 60" x 73". Five similar rose prints were used for the Rosebud blocks; the alternate blocks are quilted with a rose-and-leaf design. Quilted by Alice and Jim Graves.
(Collection of Kristy Stevens)

Weathervane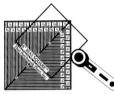

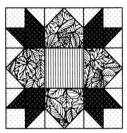

Weathervane
12" block

Dimensions: 70½" x 70½"

13 pieced blocks and 12 alternate plain blocks, 12",
set 5 across and 5 down; 1½"-wide inner border,
3½"-wide outer border.

Materials: 44"-wide fabric

3 yds. gold print for background and bias squares
1½ yds. assorted red prints for blocks
½ yd. assorted darker black prints for background
    and inner border
1¼ yds. assorted lighter black prints for
    background and outer border
4¼ yds. fabric for backing
⅝ yd. fabric for 285" of binding
Batting and thread to finish

Cutting: All measurements include ¼" seams.

From the gold and assorted red prints:

Using Cutting Format #2C (page 14), cut and
piece 4 sets of 2½"-wide bias strips to make 104
bias squares. Each set of strips will yield 33 bias
squares, 2½" x 2½". You will need 8 matching bias
squares (cut from the same red print as the
square) for each block. Edge triangles are not
used in this quilt.

From the remainder of the gold print:

Cut 52 squares, 2½" x 2½".
Cut 52 squares, 2⅞" x 2⅞". Cut diagonally to
make 104 triangles.

From the remainder of the assorted red prints:

Cut 52 squares, 2½" x 2½". Cut 4 of these
squares from the same red print as the bias
squares used in each block.

From the assorted darker black prints:

Cut 13 squares, 4½" x 4½".
Cut 8 strips, 2" x 44", for inner border.

From the assorted lighter black prints:

Cut 52 squares, 4½" x 4½". Align Bias Square®
with 3¼" marking at both sides of square and cut
away 2 corners.

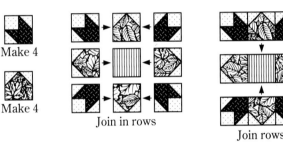

Cut 8 strips, 4" x 44", for outer borders.

DIRECTIONS

1. Piece 13 Weathervane blocks as shown.

Make 4

Make 4

Join in rows

Join rows

2. Join Weathervane blocks with alternate plain
    blocks into 5 rows of 5 blocks. Three rows will
    have 3 Weathervane blocks and two rows will
    have 2 Weathervane blocks.
3. Join rows into the quilt top.
4. Seam inner border strips together to make two
    2" x 60½" strips for sides of quilt top and two 2"
    x 63½" strips for top and bottom. Stitch inner
    borders to quilt top.
5. Seam outer border strips together to make two
    3½" x 63½" strips for sides of quilt top and two
    3½" x 70½" strips for top and bottom. Stitch
    outer borders to quilt top.
6. Layer with batting and backing; quilt or tie.

Quilting Suggestion: Quilt a feathered wreath
inside each alternate block. Outline quilt
each shape in the Weathervane block, then
quilt a diagonal grid across the quilt top to
tie the weathervane and feathered wreaths
together. Quilt the grid in the center of the
feathered wreaths but do not overlap any
quilting lines as shown on page 39.

7. Bind with straight or bias strips of fabric.

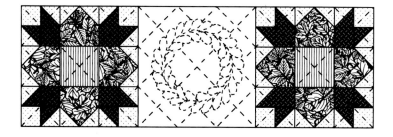

Weathervane by Nancy J. Martin, 1985, Woodinville, Washington, 70½" x 70½". A warm, gold print used in the alternate blocks highlights the delicate feather wreaths. Quilted by Andrea Scadden. (Photo by Carl Murray; collection of That Patchwork Place, Inc.)

Flock of Geese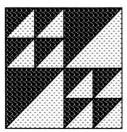

Flock of Geese
10" block

Dimensions: 58" x 78"

35 blocks, 10", set 5 across and 4 down; 4"-wide border.

Materials: 44"-wide fabric

½ yd. each of 6 different beige and tan prints
½ yd. each of 6 different blue and navy prints
1 yd. blue solid for border
3½ yds. fabric for backing
½ yd. fabric for 278" of binding
Batting and thread to finish

Cutting: All measurements include ¼" seams.

From the beige, tan, blue, and navy prints:
Using Cutting Format #3 (page 14), cut and piece 12 sets of 3"-wide bias strips to make a total of 280 bias squares. Each set of strips will yield 25 bias squares, 3" x 3". Edge triangles are not used in this quilt.

From the remainder of the beige and tan prints:
Cut 35 squares, 5⅞" x 5⅞". Cut diagonally into 70 triangles.

From the remainder of the blue and navy prints:
Cut 35 squares, 5⅞" x 5⅞". Cut diagonally into 70 triangles.

From the blue solid:
Cut 8 strips, 4" x 44", for border.

DIRECTIONS

1. Piece 35 Flock of Geese blocks as shown.

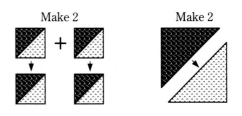

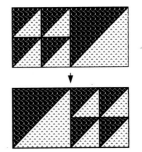

2. Join blocks together into 7 rows of 5 blocks each.
3. Join rows into the quilt top.
4. Seam border strips together to make two 4" x 70½" strips for sides of quilt and two 4" x 58" strips for top and bottom.
5. Stitch side borders to quilt top, then add borders to top and bottom.
6. Layer with batting and backing; quilt or tie.

   Quilting Suggestion: Quilt an overall pattern that does not outline the block design, such as Stock Market (page 121) or Filigree (page 127).

7. Bind with straight or bias strips of fabric.

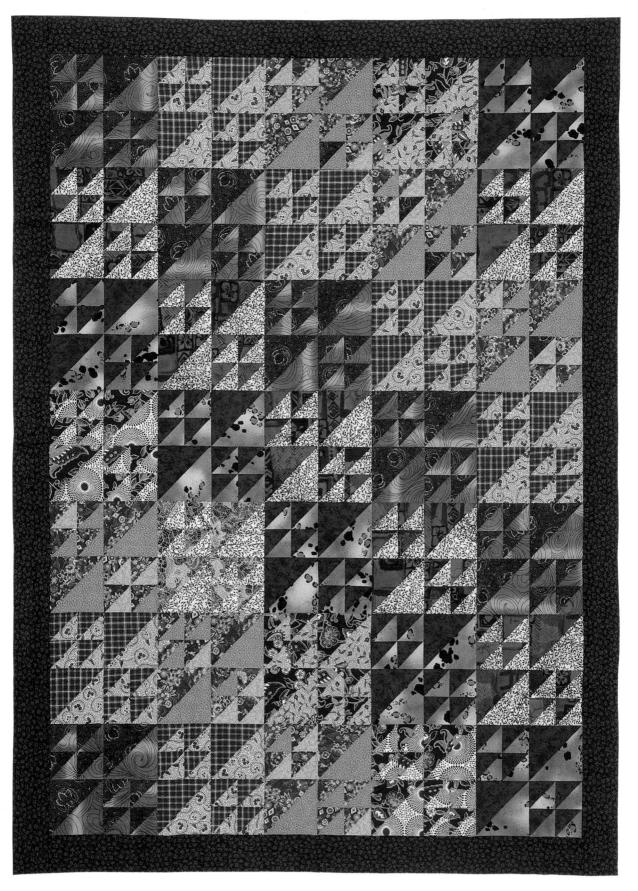

Flock of Geese by Judy Hopkins, 1991, Anchorage, Alaska, 58" x 78". This brown-and-blue quilt was made from a collection of batiklike fabrics, plus a plaid.

Double X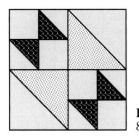

Double X
8" block

Dimensions: 40½" x 48"

24 blocks, 8", set 4 across and 6 down; 4"-wide border from strip-pieced fabric.

Materials: 44"-wide fabric

1 yd. tan print for blocks
¾ yd. black print for blocks and border
¾ yd. red print for large triangle and border
1½ yds. fabric for backing
⅜ yd. fabric for 182" of binding
Batting and thread to finish

Cutting: All measurements include ¼" seams.

From the tan and black prints:

Using Cutting Format #1D (page 13), cut and piece 3 sets of 2½"-wide bias strips to make 96 bias squares. Each set of strips will yield 35 bias squares, 2½" x 2½". Edge triangles are not used in this quilt.

From the remainder of the tan print:

Cut 96 squares, 2½" x 2½".
Cut 24 squares, 4⅞" x 4⅞". Cut diagonally into 48 triangles.

From the red print:

Cut 24 squares, 4⅞" x 4⅞". Cut diagonally into 48 triangles.
Cut 3 strips, 2½" x 44", for border.

From the remainder of the black print:

Cut 3 strips, 2½" x 44", for border.

DIRECTIONS

1. Piece 24 Double X blocks as shown.

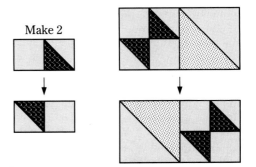

Make 2

2. Join into rows of 4 blocks each. Make 6 rows.
3. Assemble rows into quilt top.
4. Stitch strips cut from red and black fabric together. Cut into units 4½" x 4½".
5. Assemble red/black cuts into side borders. Each side border will contain 12 red/black units.
6. Attach side borders to quilt.
7. Layer with batting and backing; quilt or tie.

Quilting Suggestion: Use red perle cotton and utility quilting in an allover design, such as the Squiggly Stars (page 120). (See page 111 for information on utility quilting.)

8. Bind with straight or bias strips of fabric.

Double X by Judy Hopkins, 1991, Anchorage, Alaska, 40½" x 48". Stripped side borders add spice to this simple quilt, which was utility quilted with red perle cotton in the Squiggly Stars design.

Delectable Mountains

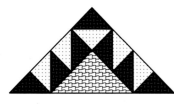

Delectable Mountains
8" x 8" x 11⅓"

Dimensions: 45¼" x 63"

20 pieced units, 8" x 8" x 11⅓", set strippy style with 4 units in each of 5 rows; 5"-wide strips between rows.

Materials: 44"-wide fabric

1½ yds. assorted light-background prints in shades of beige, tan, gray, and rust
1 yd. assorted dark prints
¾ yd. tan print for background
1½ yds. variegated striped fabric
2¾ yds. fabric for backing
½ yd. fabric for 224" of binding
Batting and thread to finish

Cutting: All measurements include ¼" seams.

From the light-background and dark prints:
Using Cutting Format #2C (page 14), cut and piece 4 sets of 2½"-wide bias strips to make a total of 100 bias squares. Each set of strips will yield 28 bias squares, 2½" x 2½". Using the 2⅞" marking on the ScrapSaver™ (page 16), resize edge triangles from dark fabric. You will need 40 dark triangles, 2 for each block. If additional half-square triangles are needed, cut a 2⅞" square diagonally.

From the remainder of the light-background prints:
Cut 5 squares, 7" x 7". Cut twice diagonally to make 20 triangles.

From the tan print:
Cut 4 squares, 12⅝" x 12⅝". Cut twice diagonally to make 15 background triangles.

Cut 5 squares, 6⅝" x 6⅝". Cut diagonally to make 10 background triangles for the ends of each row.

From the variegated striped fabric:
Cut 6 strips of fabric, 5½" x 45½".

DIRECTIONS

1. Piece 20 Delectable Mountains units as shown.

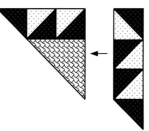

2. Join into rows with background triangles. Make 5 rows.

3. Assemble the quilt top, alternating the pieced rows with the strips of variegated striped fabric.

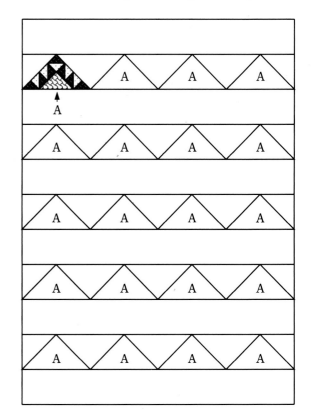

4. Layer with batting and backing; quilt or tie.

Quilting Suggestion: Outline quilt the bias squares in the Delectable Mountains units. Quilt an allover pattern, such as Hooked on Cables (page 124) or Detroit Deco (page 122), across the quilt top.

5. Bind with straight or bias strips of fabric.

Desert Storm by Terri Shinn, 1991, Anchorage, Alaska, 45¼" x 63". Delectable Mountains blocks, arranged strippy style, give this quilt a Navajo-blanket look.

London Square

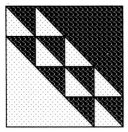

London Square
8" block

Dimensions: 48" x 64"

48 blocks, 8", set 6 across and 8 down; no border.

Materials: 44"-wide fabric

2¾ yds. tone-on-tone ivory print for blocks
2¾ yds. red print for blocks
2¾ yds. fabric for backing
½ yd. fabric for 230" of binding
Batting and thread to finish

Cutting: All measurements include ¼" seams.

From the ivory and red prints:
Using Cutting Format #1D (page 13), cut and piece 6 sets of 2½"-wide bias strips to make 192 bias squares. Each set of strips will yield 35 bias squares, 2½" x 2½". Using the 2⅞" marking on the ScrapSaver™ (page 16), resize edge triangles from the ivory and red prints. You will need 144 ivory triangles and 144 red triangles, 3 from each fabric for each block. If additional half-square triangles are needed, cut a 2⅞" square diagonally.

From the remainder of the ivory print:
Cut 24 squares, 6 ⅞" x 6⅞". Cut diagonally into 48 triangles.

From the remainder of the red print:
Cut 24 squares, 6⅞" x 6⅞". Cut diagonally into 48 triangles.

DIRECTIONS

1. Piece 48 London Square blocks as shown.

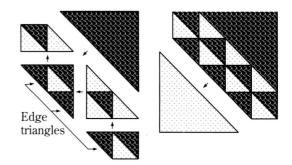

Edge triangles

2. Join into rows of 6 blocks, alternating the position of the darks and lights in each block. Make 8 rows.
3. Assemble rows into quilt top.

4. Layer with batting and backing; quilt or tie.

Quilting Suggestion: Quilt a rambling leaf pattern, such as Grape Ivy (page 125), across the quilt top.

5. Bind with straight or bias strips of fabric.

Vanilla Ice by Judy and Tom Morrison, 1991, Anchorage, Alaska, 48" x 64". Made from traditional London Square blocks in red and cream prints, this quilt is utility quilted with perle cotton in a random pattern of leaves and vines.

Birds in the Air ■

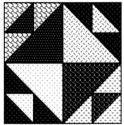

Birds in The Air
8" block

Dimensions: 45¼" x 56 ½"

31 blocks, 8", set diagonally with unpieced setting triangles and angled corners; no border.

Materials: 44"-wide fabric

1½ yds. assorted light prints for blocks
1½ yds. assorted dark prints in blue and rust for
   blocks
⅜ yd. blue print or solid-colored fabric for setting
   triangles
2¾ yds. fabric for backing
⅜ yd. fabric for 182" of binding
Batting and thread to finish

Cutting: All measurements include ¼" seams.

From the assorted light and dark prints:

Using Cutting Format #3 (page 14), cut and piece 4 sets of 2½"-wide bias strips to make 124 bias squares. Each set of strips will yield 35 bias squares, 2½" x 2½". Using the 2⅞" marking on the ScrapSaver™ (page 16), resize light and dark edge triangles. You will need 124 dark and 124 light edge triangles (4 dark and 4 light for each block). If additional half-square triangles are needed, cut a 2⅞" square diagonally.

From the remainder of the assorted light prints:

Cut 31 squares, 4⅞" x 4⅞". Cut diagonally into 62 triangles.

From the remainder of the assorted dark prints:

Cut 31 squares, 4⅞" x 4⅞". Cut diagonally into 62 triangles.

From the blue fabric for setting triangles:

Cut 3 squares, 12⅝" x 12⅝". Cut twice diagonally for 10 triangles.

DIRECTIONS

1. Piece 31 Birds in the Air blocks as shown.

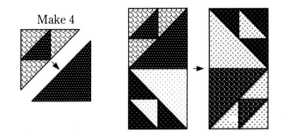

Make 4

2. Join Birds in the Air blocks into diagonal rows with setting triangles.
3. Join diagonal rows into the quilt top.

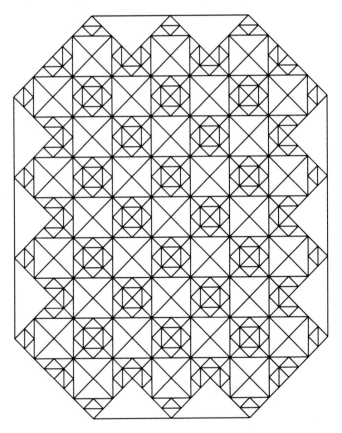

4. Layer with batting and backing; quilt or tie.

Quilting Suggestion: Quilt ¼" inside each large and small triangle.

5. Bind with straight or bias strips of fabric.

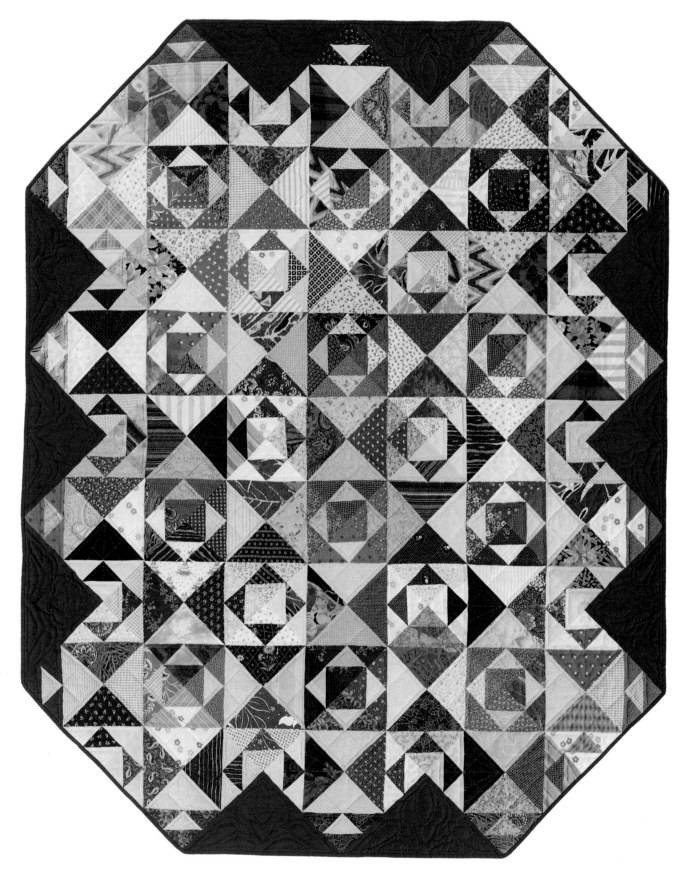

Hidden Stars by Louise Bremner, 1989, Anchorage, Alaska, 45¼" x 56½". Classic Birds in the Air blocks, arranged on point, form hidden stars.

Scrap Angles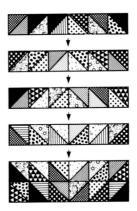

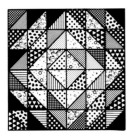

Scrap Angles
12" block

Dimensions: 48" x 72"

24 blocks, 12", set 6 across and 4 down; no border.

Materials: 44"-wide fabric

2 yds. assorted light prints for blocks
2 yds. assorted medium prints for blocks
2 yds. assorted dark prints for blocks
2¾ yds. fabric for backing
½ yd. dark fabric for 250" of binding
Batting and thread to finish

Cutting: All measurements include ¼" seams.

From the assorted light, medium, and dark prints:
Using Format #3 (page 14), cut and piece 25 sets of 2½"-wide bias strips to make 864 bias squares. Each set of strips will yield 35 bias squares, 2½" x 2½". Edge triangles are not used in this quilt.

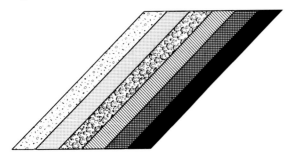

DIRECTIONS

1. Piece 24 Scrap Angles blocks as shown. Beginning at the block center, arrange the bias squares in each block from light to medium to dark.

2. Join Scrap Angles blocks into rows of 6 blocks. Make 4 rows.
3. Assemble rows into the quilt top.

4. Layer with batting and backing; quilt or tie.

   Quilting Suggestion: Quilt a diagonal grid pattern across the quilt.

5. Bind with straight or bias strips of fabric.

Scrap Angles by Paulette Peters, 1988, Elkhorn, Nebraska, 48″ x 72″. Made as a color study, this wonderful scrap quilt incorporates a wide variety of prints. (Photo courtesy of Myron Miller, © 1990)

Friendship Star

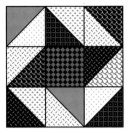

Friendship Star
6" block

Dimensions: 58" x 72"

99 blocks, 6", set 9 across and 11 down; 2"-wide pieced border.

Materials: 44"-wide fabric

2 yds. assorted light prints for blocks
2 yds. assorted medium prints for blocks
2½ yds. assorted dark prints for blocks
3⅜ yds. fabric for backing
½ yd. dark fabric for 268" of binding
Batting and thread to finish

Cutting: All measurements include ¼" seams.

From the assorted light, medium, and dark prints:
  Using Cutting Format #3 (page 14), cut and piece 25 sets of 2½"-wide bias strips to make 872 bias squares. Each set of strips will yield 35 bias squares, 2½" x 2½". Edge triangles are not used in this quilt.

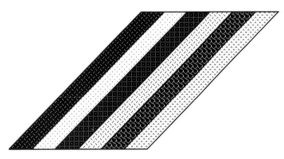

From the remainder of the dark prints:
  Cut 143 squares, 2½" x 2½".

DIRECTIONS

1. Piece 99 Friendship Star blocks as shown.

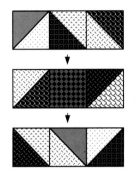

2. Join Friendship Star blocks into rows of 9 blocks. Make 11 rows.
3. Assemble rows into the quilt top.
4. Use remaining bias squares and cut fabric squares for the pieced border.
   a. Piece a border unit for each side, using 22 bias squares and 11 squares cut from dark prints for each unit.

   b. Piece a border unit for top and bottom, using 18 bias squares and 11 squares cut from dark prints for each unit..

5. Stitch border units to sides, then stitch border units to top and bottom.
6. Layer with batting and backing; quilt or tie.

   Quilting Suggestion: Outline the center portion of each star. Then, quilt diagonal lines in the light fabrics surrounding each star. Quilt ¼" inside the remaining diamond shape.

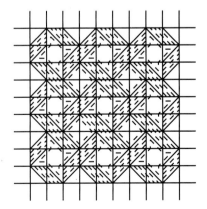

7. Bind with straight or bias strips of fabric.

Harmony by Paulette Peters, 1989, Elkhorn, Nebraska, 58" x 72". This Friendship Star variation made from gathered scraps symbolizes the interconnectedness of generations of women and the friendships that evolved through quilting. (Photo courtesy of Myron Miller, © 1990)

Indian Trails

Indian Trails
16" block

Dimensions: 56" x 74"

12 blocks, 16", set 3 across and 4 down with 2"-wide sashing; 4"-wide border.

Materials: 44"-wide fabric

2 yds. assorted light plaids or checks for background
2 yds. black and blue solids for bias squares and sashing
2½ yds. assorted black, brown, blue, and pink plaids for triangles
1 yd. blue solid for border (cut crosswise)
3½ yds. fabric for backing
½ yd. fabric for 280" of binding
Batting and thread to finish

Cutting: All measurements include ¼" seams.

From the assorted light plaids and black solid:
Using Cutting Format #3 (page 14), cut and piece 9 sets of 2½"-wide bias strips to make 288 bias squares. Each set of strips will yield 35 bias squares, 2½" x 2½". Edge triangles are not used in this quilt.

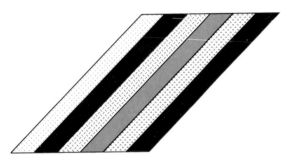

From the assorted black, brown, blue, and pink plaids:
Cut 48 squares, 6⅞" x 6⅞". Cut diagonally into 96 triangles.

From the remainder of the black solid:
Cut 8 strips, 2½" x 16½", for sashing.
Cut 3 strips, 2½" x 70½", for sashing.

From the blue solid:
Cut 8 strips, 2½" x 44", for borders.

DIRECTIONS

1. Piece 12 Indian Trails blocks as shown.

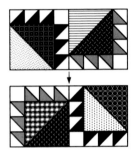

Make 4

2. Piece 4 rows, using 3 blocks and 2 sashing pieces for each row.
3. Assemble rows of blocks with long sashing strips between them to form quilt top.
4. Seam border strips cut from blue solid to make two 2½" x 70½" strips for sides of quilt top and two 2½" x 60½" strips for top and bottom.
5. Layer with batting and backing; quilt or tie.

   Quilting Suggestion: Quilt ¼" away from edges inside all light fabrics used on outer edges of bias squares. Quilt ½" away from edges inside all the larger triangles. Quilt ¼" away from edges on sashing.

6. Bind with straight or bias strips of fabric.

Indian Trails by Evelyn Bright, 1991, Bremerton, Washington, 56" x 74". A lively quilt, featuring plaids and stripes, is accented by a bold black in the bias squares and sashing.
(Photo by Brian Kaplan)

Stardancer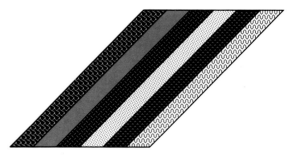

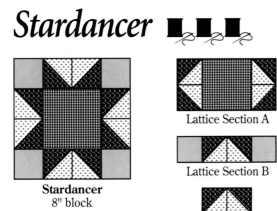

Stardancer
8" block

Lattice Section A

Lattice Section B

Lattice Section C

Dimensions: 92" x 104"

48 blocks, 8", set 6 across and 8 down with pieced lattices that form 49 stars in lattice; 6"-wide pieced border.

Materials: 44"-wide fabric

1½ yds. assorted tan prints for triangles
2 yds. dark blue print for star tips
2 yds. contrasting brown, gold, red, and green prints for lattice
2 yds. assorted light solids for corners
1½ yds. assorted light blue prints for star centers
8 yds. fabric for backing
¾ yd. fabric for 392" of binding
Batting and thread to finish

Cutting: All measurements include ¼" seams.

From the assorted tan and dark blue prints:
Using Cutting Format #2D (page 14), cut and piece 11 sets of 2½"-wide bias strips to make 384 bias squares. Each set of strips will yield 35 bias squares, 2½" x 2½". You will need 8 matching bias squares for each blue star block. Edge triangles are not used in this quilt.

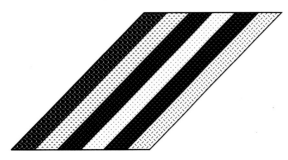

From the contrasting (brown, gold, red, and green) and tan prints:
Using Cutting Format #2D (page 14), cut and piece 14 sets of 2½"-wide bias strips to make 460 bias squares. Each set of strips will yield 35 bias squares, 2½" x 2½". You will need 8 matching bias squares for the pieced lattices that form contrasting stars.

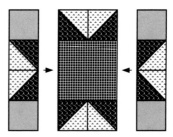

From the assorted light solids:
Cut 224 squares, 2½" x 2½".

From the assorted light blue prints:
Cut 48 squares, 4½" x 4½".

From the remainder of the contrasting prints:
Cut 149 squares, 4½" x 4½", for lattice.

For the pieced border:
Cut 8 strips, 2" x 44", from light blue, dark blue, gold, brown, light red, and deep red prints.
Cut 16 strips, 2" x 44", from tan prints.
Cut 2 light red squares, 4⅞" x 4⅞". Cut diagonally to make 4 triangles.
Cut 2 dark red squares, 4⅞" x 4⅞". Cut diagonally to make 4 triangles.

DIRECTIONS

1. Piece 48 Sawtooth Star blocks as shown, using light blue fabric for star centers and dark blue fabric for star tips.

2. Piece 100 Lattice Section A, 16 Lattice Section B, and 14 Lattice Section C, using the bias squares cut from the assorted contrasting (brown, gold, red, and green) and tan prints.

SuzAnn Hull Quilt by Byrd Tribble, 1988, Coral Gables, Florida, 92" x 104". Byrd added some of her own fabrics and those contributed by friends to a carton of scraps that SuzAnn Hull was about to donate to a thrift shop. The carton contained some wonderful batiks as well as Indian and European cottons. The pieced border was Byrd's addition to the original Stardancer© quilt designed by Marsha McCloskey.

3. Join 6 Stardancer blocks with 7 Lattice Section A and 2 Lattice Section B to form a row. Make 8 rows.

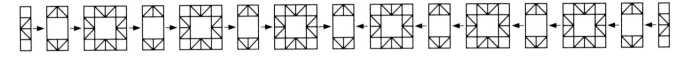

4. Alternate seven 4½" x 4½" squares of contrasting prints cut for lattice with 6 Lattice Section B units to form a row. Add 2 Lattice Section C to the end of each row. Make 7 rows.

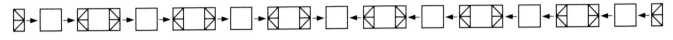

5. Set top together, alternating rows of Sawtooth Star blocks and lattice rows.

6. The pieced border has a three-dimensional look achieved by the fabric placement in the chevron units. To make chevrons, make 8 each of the strip units shown below. Cut units diagonally, using the 45° angle marking every 2½".

Tan
Dark blue
Brown
Dark red

Tan
Light blue
Gold
Light red

7. To piece border:
   a. Alternate light and dark strip units to form chevrons. Piece 23 chevrons into border units for each side.
   b. Alternate 20 light and 20 dark strips to form chevron border units for top and bottom.
   c. Trim border units ¼" away from points.
   d. Add a corner unit to each end of border unit for top and bottom.

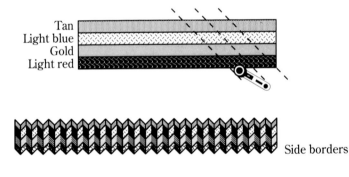

Side borders

Top and bottom borders

Corner unit

8. Stitch border units to sides, then stitch border units to top and bottom.

9. Layer with batting and backing; quilt or tie.

Quilting Suggestion: Quilt with an overall pattern, such as Baptist Fan (page 22) or Squiggly Stars (page 120).

10. Bind with straight or bias strips of fabric.

Double Ninepatch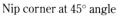

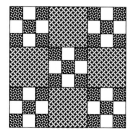

Double Ninepatch
9" block

Dimensions: 90" x 90"

41 Double Ninepatch blocks, 9", set on point with 3"-wide sashing and Ninepatch sashing squares; 4½"-wide border.

Materials: 44"-wide fabric

2¼ yds. assorted dark blue prints for Ninepatch blocks
1¾ yds. assorted white prints for Ninepatch blocks
1⅝ yds. red print for alternate blocks
2½ yds. navy blue print for side triangles and seamed border
2⅔ yds. pink print for sashing and corner triangles
8 yds. fabric for backing
¾ yd. fabric for 378" of narrow binding
Batting and thread to finish

Cutting: All measurements include ¼" seams.

From the assorted dark blue prints:
Cut 50 strips, 1½" x 44", for blocks.

From the assorted white prints:
Cut 40 strips, 1½" x 44", for blocks.

From the red print:
Cut 15 strips, 3½" x 44". Cut the strips into 164 squares, 3½" x 3½", for alternate blocks.

From the navy blue print:
Cut 12 strips, 5" x 44", for seamed border.
Cut 4 squares, 14" x 14". Cut twice diagonally into 16 quarter-square triangles for sides.

Note: Side and corner triangles may be larger than needed. Trim *after* quilt top is assembled.

From the pink print:
Cut 2 squares, 7¼" x 7¼". Cut diagonally into 4 half-square triangles for corners.

Cut 16 strips, 3½" x 44". Cut the strips into 64 rectangles, 3½" x 9½", for sashing.
Cut 8 strips, 3½" x 44". Cut the strips into 32 rectangles, 3½" x 9⅞". Nip one corner of each rectangle at a 45° angle as shown, making 16 Shape A and 16 Shape B for outer sashing pieces.

Nip corner at 45° angle

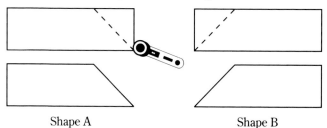

Shape A   Shape B

DIRECTIONS

1. Join 40 of the dark blue and 20 of the white strips to make 20 strip units as shown. The units should measure 3½" wide when sewn. Cut the units into 490 segments, 1½" wide.

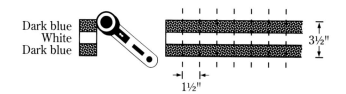

2. Join the remaining dark blue and white strips to make 10 strip units as shown. The units should measure 3½" wide when sewn. Cut the units into 245 segments, 1½" wide.

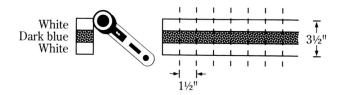

3. Join the segments into 245 Ninepatch units.

4. Join 205 of the Ninepatch units with the 3½" red squares to make 41 Double Ninepatch blocks. The remaining 40 Ninepatch units will be used for sashing squares.

5. Set the blocks together in diagonal rows with the pink sashing pieces, Ninepatch sashing squares, pink corner triangles, and navy blue side triangles as shown. Join the rows. Trim and square up the outside edges after the quilt top has been assembled, if needed; be sure to leave ¼" seam allowances all around. To set blocks on point, see "Assembling On-Point Quilts," page 106.

6. Add border: Seam the navy blue strips to make strips long enough to border the quilt. See page 108 for information on attaching straight-cut borders.

7. Layer with batting and backing; quilt or tie.

Quilting Suggestion: Quilt concentric squares in the blocks and straight lines in the sashing as shown; use a curvy cable or vine in the border.

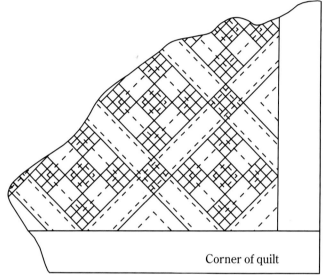

Corner of quilt

8. Bind with straight or bias strips of fabric.

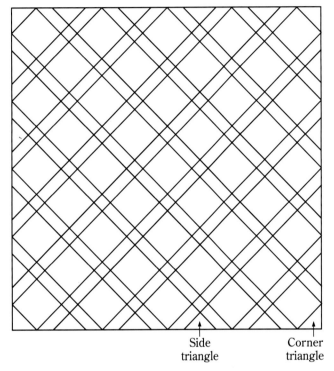

Side
triangle

Corner
triangle

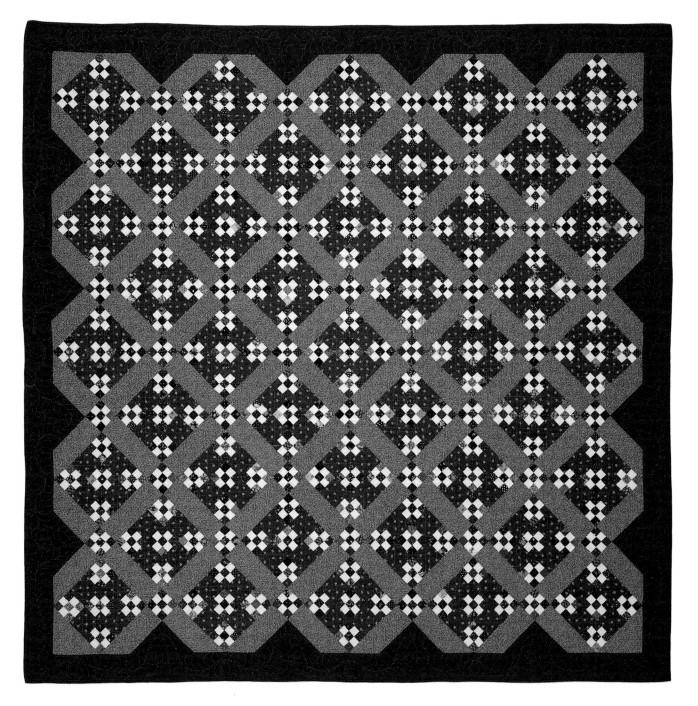

Double Ninepatch by Donna Hanson Eines, 1988, Edmonds, Washington, 90" x 90".
This lovely quilt features brightly colored scraps inside pink sashing. The solid navy border highlights
the beautiful feathered quilting design.

Rail Fence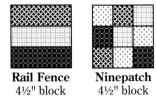

Rail Fence
4½" block

Ninepatch
4½" block

Dimensions: 54" x 63"

120 blocks, 4½", set 10 across and 12 down; 1½"-wide inner border; 3"-wide outer border with corner squares.

Materials: 44"-wide fabric

2¾ yds. assorted red, purple, and gold prints for blocks
½ yd. bright purple print for seamed inner border
⅞ yd. hot pink print for seamed outer border
¼ yd. red print for border corners
3⅜ yds. fabric for backing
½ yd. fabric for 252" of narrow binding
Batting and thread to finish

Cutting: All measurements include ¼" seams.

From the assorted red, purple, and gold prints:
Cut 48 strips, 2" x 44", for blocks. Cut each strip in half to yield 96 strips, 2" x 22".

From the bright purple print:
Cut 8 strips, 2" x 44", for the seamed inner border.

From the hot pink print:
Cut 8 strips, 3½" x 44", for the seamed outer border.

From the red print:
Cut 4 squares, 5" x 5", for border corners.

DIRECTIONS

1. Join the 2" x 22" strips at random to make 32 strip units as shown. The units should measure 5" wide when sewn. Cut 28 units into segments 5" wide to make 112 Rail Fence blocks.

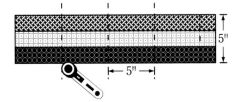

2. From the remaining strip units, cut 24 segments, 2" wide. Join these segments at random into 8 Ninepatch blocks.

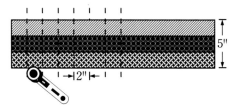

3. Set the blocks together in rows of 10 as shown in the photo, distributing the Ninepatch blocks at random; join the rows.

4. Add borders: Seam the bright purple and hot pink strips as necessary to make strips long enough to border the quilt. Join the purple and hot pink strips into 4 stripped border pieces, staggering the seams. Measure the length and the width of the quilt at the center. Cut 2 of the stripped border pieces to the lengthwise measurement and join to the sides of the quilt. Cut the 2 remaining stripped border pieces to the original crosswise measurement, join the red corner squares to the ends of the strips, and stitch to the top and bottom.

5. Layer with batting and backing; quilt or tie.

Quilting Suggestion: The quilt shown in the photo is finished with the Mennonite Tack (page 112), using perle cotton. As an alternative, consider block-oriented, straight-line quilting through the center of each "rail" as shown below, or use a curvy allover repeat design like Squiggly Stars (page 120).

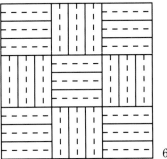

6 blocks

6. Bind with straight or bias strips of fabric.

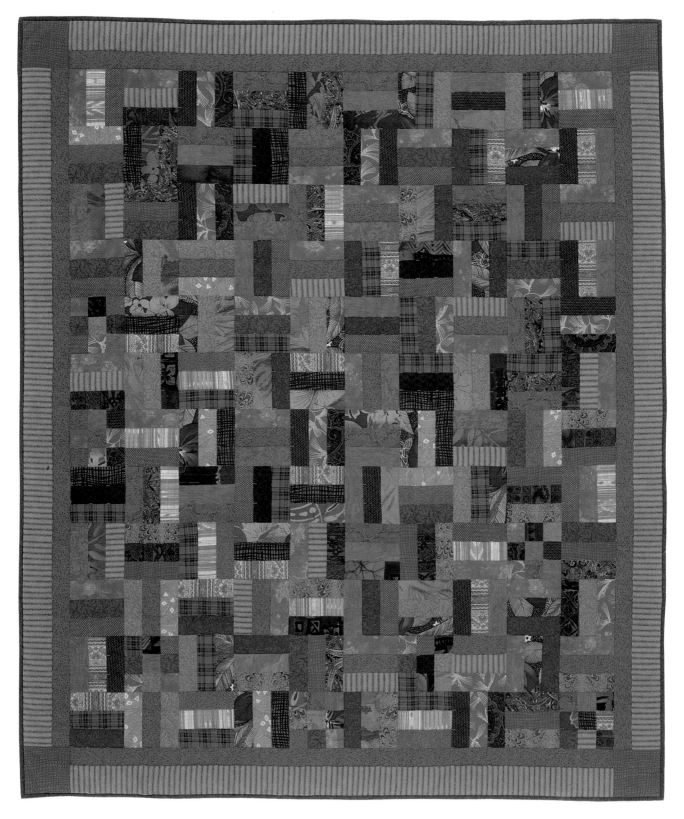

Sunset Strip by Judy Hopkins, 1991, Anchorage, Alaska, 54″ x 63″. Traditional Rail Fence blocks in hot pinks, reds, and purples are joined by a few Ninepatch blocks. The quilt is finished with the Mennonite Tack.

Paths and Stiles ◼️◼️

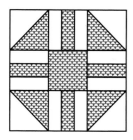

Paths and Stiles
9" block

Dimensions: 80" x 86"

42 blocks, 9", set 7 across and 6 down with 3"-wide sashing strips; 3"-wide inner border; 3"-wide second border; 2½"-wide outer border.

Materials: 44"-wide fabric

4½ yds. assorted pink-on-pink prints for blocks and seamed border
6½ yds. light print for blocks and seamed borders
5¼ yds. fabric for backing
⅝ yd. fabric for 350" of narrow binding
Batting and thread to finish

Cutting: All measurements include ¼" seams.

From the pink-on-pink and light prints:

Using Cutting Format #1D (page 13), cut and piece 7 sets of 3½"-wide bias strips to make 168 bias squares. Each set of strips will yield 25 bias squares, 3½" x 3½". Edge triangles are not used in this quilt.

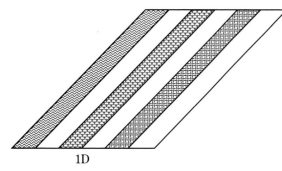

1D

From the remainder of the pink-on-pink prints:

Cut 16 strips, 1½" x 44", for blocks.
Cut 4 strips, 3½" x 44". Cut the strips into 42 squares, 3½" x 3½", for blocks.
Cut 9 strips, 3½" x 44", for seamed second border.

From the remainder of the light print:

Cut 32 strips, 1½" x 44", for blocks.
Cut 10 strips, 3½" x 44", for seamed sashing.
Cut 8 strips, 3½" x 44", for seamed inner border.
Cut 9 strips, 3" x 44", for seamed outer border.

DIRECTIONS

1. Join the 1½" x 44" pink and light print strips to make 16 strip units as shown. The units should measure 3½" wide when sewn. Cut the units into 168 segments, 3½" wide.

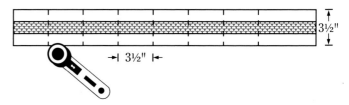

2. Piece 42 Paths and Stiles blocks as shown.

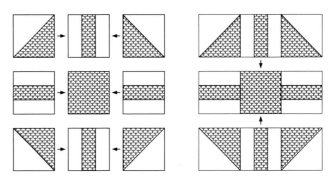

3. Set the blocks together in rows of 7. Seam the sashing strips as necessary and join the rows, adding a sashing strip between each row as shown in the photo.
4. Add inner border: Seam the 3½" x 44" light print strips as necessary to make strips long enough to border the quilt. See page 108 for information on attaching straight-cut borders.
5. Add second border: Seam the 3½" x 44" pink strips as necessary. Join to the quilt as for inner border.
6. Add outer border: Seam the 3" x 44" light print strips as necessary. Join to the quilt as for previous borders.
7. Layer with batting and backing; quilt or tie.

Quilting Suggestion: Emphasize the circular look of the block by quilting concentric circles in the blocks and concentric diamonds in the spaces between the blocks as shown.

8. Bind with straight or bias strips of fabric.

4 blocks

Paths and Stiles, maker unknown, c. 1920, Pennsylvania, 80" x 86". A vintage collection of double-pink prints are used for this variation of Paths and Stiles, an early Nancy Cabot pattern. (Collection of Nancy J. Martin)

Shaded Ninepatch

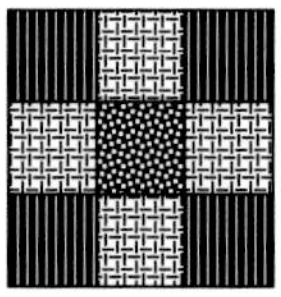

Ninepatch A	Ninepatch B	Block C
6" block	6" block	6" block

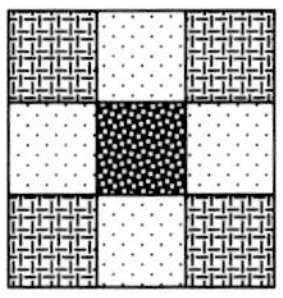

Dimensions: 76" x 76"

50 Ninepatch blocks and 50 half-square triangle blocks, each 6" square, set 10 across and 10 down; 2"-wide inner border; 6"-wide outer border.

Materials: 44"-wide fabric

1¼ yds. assorted light red prints for Ninepatch blocks

⅞ yd. assorted dark brown and gray prints for Ninepatch blocks

⅓ yd. light print for Ninepatch blocks

1⅞ yds. green print for Ninepatch blocks and seamed outer border

1 yd. pink print for half-square triangle blocks

1 yd. gray solid for half-square triangle blocks

⅝ yd. yellow print for seamed inner border

4⅝ yds. fabric for backing

⅝ yd. fabric for 322" of narrow binding

Batting and thread to finish

Cutting: All measurements include ¼" seams.

From the assorted light red prints:
Cut 16 strips, 2½" x 44", for Ninepatch blocks.

From the assorted dark brown and gray prints:
Cut 12 strips, 2½" x 44", for Ninepatch blocks.

From the light print:
Cut 4 strips, 2½" x 44", for Ninepatch blocks.

From the green print:
Cut 4 strips, 2½" x 44", for Ninepatch blocks.
Cut 8 strips, 6½" x 44", for seamed outer border.

From the pink print:
Cut 5 strips, 6⅞" x 44". Cut the strips into 25 squares, 6⅞" x 6⅞". Cut diagonally into 50 half-square triangles for alternate blocks.

From the gray solid:
Cut 5 strips, 6⅞" x 44". Cut the strips into 25 squares, 6⅞" x 6⅞". Cut diagonally into 50 half-square triangles for alternate blocks.

From the yellow print:
Cut 8 strips, 2½" x 44", for seamed inner border.

DIRECTIONS

1. Join 6 of the assorted light red strips and 3 of the green strips to make 3 strip units as shown. The units should measure 6½" wide when sewn. Cut the units into 40 segments, 2½" wide.

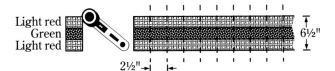

2. Join the dark brown and gray strips and 6 of the assorted light red strips to make 6 strip units as shown. The units should measure 6½" wide when sewn. Cut into 80 segments, 2½" wide.

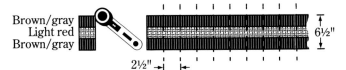

3. Join the segments into 40 Ninepatch Block A.

4. Join 2 of the light print strips and the remaining green strip to make 1 strip unit as shown. The unit should measure 6½" wide when sewn. Cut the unit into 10 segments, 2½" wide.

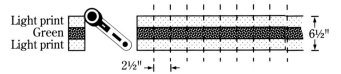

5. Join the remaining light red and light print strips into 2 strip units as shown. The units should measure 6½" wide when sewn. Cut the units into 20 segments, 2½" wide.

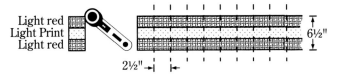

6. Join the segments into 10 Ninepatch Block B.

7. Join the pink and gray triangles into 50 Block C.

8. Set the blocks together in rows of 10 as shown in the photo, alternating Ninepatch and half-square triangle blocks; join the rows.

9. Add inner border: Seam the yellow strips as necessary to make strips long enough to border the quilt. See page 108 for information on attaching straight-cut borders.

10. Add outer border: Seam the 6½" green strips as necessary. Measure and join to the quilt as for inner border.

11. Layer with batting and backing; quilt or tie.

Quilting Suggestion: Consider block-oriented diagonal lines as shown, or try a linear repeat pattern like Stock Market (page 121). For this quilt, setting the Stock Market pattern on the diagonal would be effective.

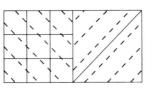

2 blocks

12. Bind with straight or bias strips of fabric.

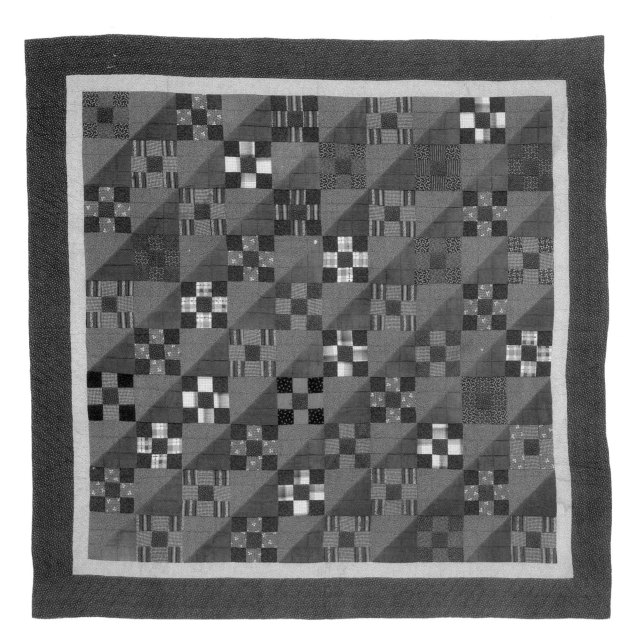

Shaded Ninepatch, maker unknown, c. 1920, Pennsylvania, 76" x 76". The green center squares in these simple Ninepatch blocks, which are made from many dark fabric scraps, unify the quilt. The alternate blocks of pink and gray triangles also tie the quilt together and create a feeling of movement. (Collection of Nancy J. Martin)

Magic Carpet ◾◼

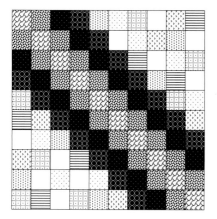

Magic Carpet
15" block

Dimensions: 60" x 81"

20 blocks, 15", set 5 across and 4 down; 3"-wide top and bottom borders.

Materials: 44"-wide fabric

⅝ yd. yellow print for blocks
1⅛ yds. pink or light red print for blocks
1 yd. black print for blocks
⅞ yd. red print for blocks
3½ yds. assorted neutral prints for blocks (Try ¼ yd. each of 14 different fabrics.)
½ yd. black or gray print for seamed borders
3¾ yds. fabric for backing
⅝ yd. fabric for 300" of narrow binding
Batting and thread to finish

Cutting: All measurements include ¼" seams.

From the yellow print:
Cut 10 strips, 2" x 44", for blocks.

From the pink or light red print:
Cut 18 strips, 2" x 44", for blocks.

From the black print:
Cut 16 strips, 2" x 44", for blocks.

From the red print:
Cut 14 strips, 2" x 44", for blocks.

From the assorted neutral prints:
Cut 42 strips, 2" x 44" (3 strips from each fabric), for blocks.

From the black or gray print:
Cut 4 strips, 3½" x 44", for seamed top and bottom borders.

DIRECTIONS

1. Join the 2" x 44" strips into strip units as shown. Make 2 Unit A, 2 Unit B, and so on, for a total of 10 strip units. Each unit uses 10 strips; the units should measure 15½" wide when sewn.

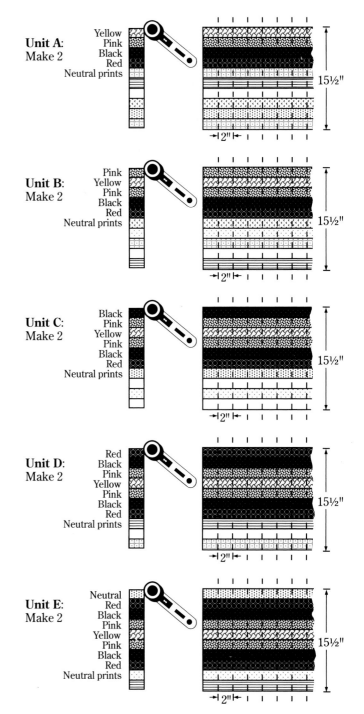

2. Cut each strip unit into 20 segments, 2" wide; join the segments into 20 Magic Carpet blocks. Each block uses 2 segments from each unit.

3. Set the blocks together in rows of 5 as shown in the photo; join the rows.

4. Add borders: Seam the 3½" x 44" black or gray strips as necessary to make strips long enough to border the top and bottom edges of the quilt. See page 108 for information on attaching straight-cut borders.

5. Layer with batting and backing; quilt or tie.

Quilting Suggestion: Crow footing (page 111) is speedy and would add an interesting dimension to this quilt; put a stitch in the center of each small square. As an alternative, try an allover diagonal grid, avoiding the layers of seams at the corners as shown.

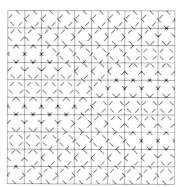

1 block

6. Bind with straight or bias strips of fabric.

Magic Carpet, maker unknown, c. 1900, Pennsylvania, 60" x 81". This well-worn treasure features several repeating fabrics in the twenty identical blocks. Create a contemporary version quickly and easily by using strip-piecing techniques. (Collection of Nancy J. Martin)

Ann Orr's Rose Garden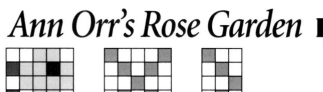

| Block A 8¾" | Block B 8¾" | Block C 5¼" x 8¾" |

Dimensions: 82¼" x 82¼"

49 blocks, 8¾", set 7 across and 7 down with partial blocks at the outside edges; 1¾"-wide inner border; 3½"-wide outer border.

Materials: 44"-wide fabric

5¼ yds. muslin print for blocks and seamed outer border
2 yds. pink solid for blocks and seamed inner border
¼ yd. dark pink solid for blocks
⅝ yd. green print for blocks
1¼ yds. blue print for blocks
5 yds. fabric for backing
⅝ yd. fabric for 347" of narrow binding
Batting and thread to finish

Cutting: All measurements include ¼" seams.

From the *muslin* print:
    Cut 54 strips, 2¼" x 44", for blocks.
    Cut 10 strips, 4" x 44", for seamed outer border.
    Cut 4 strips, 5¾" x 44". Cut the strips into 12 rectangles, 5¾" x 9¼", for sides, *and* 4 squares, 5¾" x 5¾", for corners.

From the pink solid:
    Cut 22 strips, 2¼" x 44", for blocks.
    Cut 8 strips, 2¼" x 44", for inner border.

From the dark pink solid:
    Cut 2 strips, 2¼" x 44", for blocks.

From the green print:
    Cut 8 strips, 2¼" x 44", for blocks.

From the blue print:
    Cut 19 strips, 2¼" x 44", for blocks.

DIRECTIONS

1. Join the 2¼" x 44" muslin, pink, dark pink, and green strips into strip units as shown. Make 2 Unit A, 2 Unit B, and so on, for a total of 10 strip units. The units should measure 9¼" wide

when sewn. Cut 25 segments, 2¼" wide, from Unit A, 25 from Unit B, and so on; join the segments into 25 Block A.

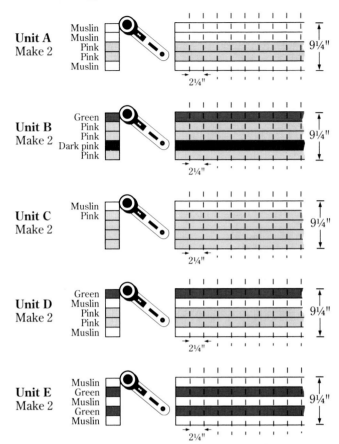

2. Join the 2¼" x 44" muslin and blue strips into strip units as shown. Make 4 Unit F, 4 Unit G, and 3 Unit H. The units should measure 9¼" wide when sewn. Cut 64 segments, 2¼" wide, from Unit F; 64 segments, 2¼" wide, from Unit G; and 40 segments, 2¼" wide, from Unit H. Join the segments into 24 Block B and 16 Block C.

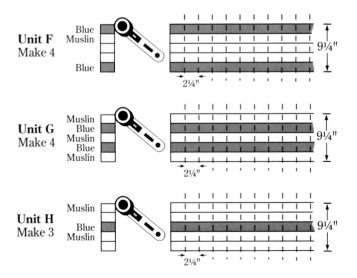

3. Set the blocks and the muslin squares and rectangles together into 4 Row A, 3 Row B, and 2 Row C as shown.

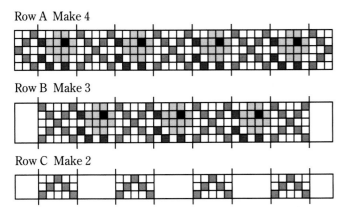

Row A Make 4

Row B Make 3

Row C Make 2

4. Join the A and B rows, starting with Row A and alternating A and B. Add a C row to the top and bottom of the quilt, completing the blue "chain" as shown in the photo.

5. Add inner border: Seam the remaining 2¼" x 44" pink strips as necessary to make strips long enough to border the quilt. See page 108 for information on attaching straight-cut borders.

6. Add outer border: Seam the 4" x 44" muslin strips and join to the quilt as for inner border.

7. Layer with batting and backing; quilt or tie.

Quilting Suggestion: Because this quilt has so many seams, crow footing (page 111) would be a good finishing technique; put a stitch in the center of each small square. Or, consider a delicate, allover design like Filigree (page 127) or a diagonal grid that avoids the layers of seams at the corners as shown for the Magic Carpet quilt on page 69.

8. Bind with straight or bias strips of fabric.

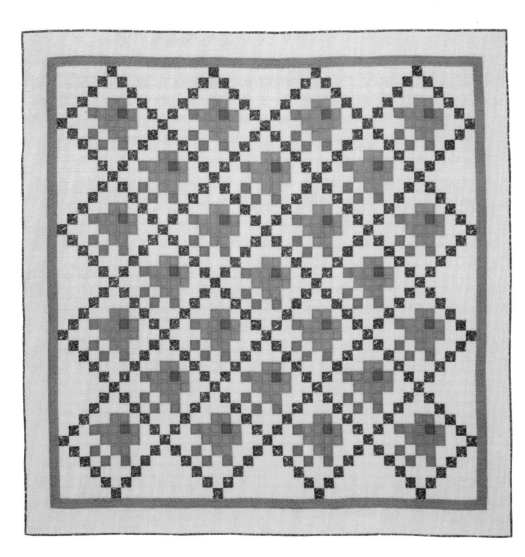

Anne Orr's Rose Garden by Mimi Dietrich, 1989, Catonsville, Maryland, 82¼" x 82¼". Inspired by the design on an antique quilt, Mimi recreated this pleasing top, which combines Rose and Single Irish Chain blocks. It is reminiscent of the Anne Orr designs created during the 1930s.

Cracker Box

Block A
11¾"

Block B
11¾"

Dimensions: 60" x 94"

40 blocks, 11¾", set 5 across and 8 down; no border.

Materials: 44"-wide fabric

3 yds. muslin or light print fabric
½ yd. each of 5 different medium prints
⅓ yd. each of 5 different dark prints
5⅝ yds. fabric for backing
⅝ yd. fabric for 326" of narrow binding
Batting and thread to finish

Cutting: All measurements include ¼" seams.

From the muslin or light print:
    Cut 15 strips, 3¼" x 44".
    Cut 8 strips, 6¾" x 44". Cut the strips into 40 squares, 6¾" x 6¾". Cut diagonally into 80 half-square triangles.

From *each* of the 5 medium prints:
    Cut 2 strips, 3¼" x 44".
    Cut 1 strip, 6¾" x 44". Cut the strip into 4 squares, 6¾" x 6¾". Cut diagonally into 8 half-square triangles.

From *each* of the 5 dark prints:
    Cut 1 strip, 3¼" x 44".
    Cut 1 strip, 6¾" x 44". Cut the strip into 4 squares, 6¾" x 6¾". Cut diagonally into 8 half-square triangles.

DIRECTIONS

1. Join 5 of the muslin strips with the 10 medium strips to make 5 strip units as shown. Use the same medium fabric for the 2 outer strips in each unit. The units should measure 8¾" wide when sewn. Cut the units into 20 segments, 8¾" wide.

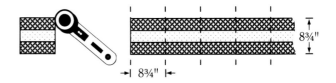

2. Add muslin and medium triangles to the segments to make 20 Block A, matching the medium triangles to the medium fabric in the strip segments.

3. Join the remaining muslin strips with the 5 dark strips to make 5 strip units as shown. The units should measure 8¾" wide when sewn. Cut the units into 20 segments, 8¾" wide.

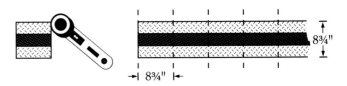

4. Add muslin and dark triangles to the segments to make 20 Block B as shown, matching dark triangles to dark fabric in the strip segments.

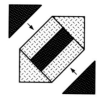

5. Set the blocks together in rows of 5 as shown in the photo, using only Block A in 4 of the rows and only Block B in the other 4 rows. Join the rows, alternating those that contain Block A with those that contain Block B.

6. Layer with batting and backing; quilt or tie.

Quilting Suggestion: The quilt shown in the photo is quilted with block-oriented diagonal lines as shown. As an alternative, consider an allover pattern, like Detroit Deco (page 122), running on the diagonal.

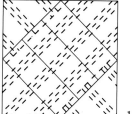

1 block

7. Bind with straight or bias strips of fabric.

Cracker Box by Della Currier Riley and Bernice Riley Smalley, 1952, Washington, 60" x 94". Bernice Smalley finished the piecing and quilting begun by her mother, Della Currier Riley, after Della's death. The pattern is named for its shape, which resembles party crackers, the little packets filled with treats and tied together at each end.

Buckeye Beauty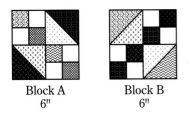

Block A
6"

Block B
6"

Dimensions: 66" x 84"

130 blocks, 6", set 13 across and 13 down; 3"-wide border.

Materials: 44"-wide fabric

5½ yds. assorted light prints for blocks
2¾ yds. assorted medium gray and tan prints for blocks
2¾ yds. assorted red and black prints for blocks
⅞ yd. black print for seamed border
4 yds. fabric for backing
⅝ yd. fabric for 318" of narrow binding
Batting and thread to finish

Cutting: All measurements include ¼" seams.

From the light and medium prints:
Using Cutting Format #2C (page 14), cut and piece 7 sets of 3½"-wide bias strips to make 130 light/medium bias squares. Each set of strips will yield 20 bias squares, 3½" x 3½".

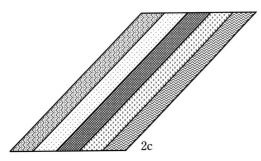

2c

From the light prints and the red and black prints:
Using Cutting Format #2C (page 14), cut and piece 7 sets of 3½"-wide bias strips to make 130 light/dark bias squares. Each set of strips will yield 20 bias squares, 3½" x 3½".

From the remainder of the light prints:
Cut 26 strips, 2" x 44", for blocks.

From the remainder of the medium prints:
Cut 13 strips, 2" x 44", for blocks.

From the remainder of the red and black prints:
Cut 13 strips, 2" x 44", for blocks.

From the black print:
Cut 8 strips, 3½" x 44", for seamed border.

DIRECTIONS

1. Join the medium gray and tan strips to 13 of the light strips to make 13 strip units as shown. The units should measure 3½" wide when sewn. Cut the units into 260 segments, 2" wide.

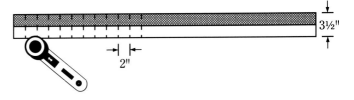

2. Join the segments into 130 light/medium Four Patches as shown.

3. Join the red and black strips to the remaining light strips to make 13 strip units. The units should measure 3½" wide when sewn. Cut the units into 260 segments, 2" wide. Join the segments into 130 light/dark Four Patches.

4. Piece 65 Block A, using the light/medium Four Patches and the light/dark bias squares; then, piece 65 Block B, using the light/dark Four Patches and the light/medium bias squares.

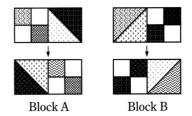

Block A   Block B

5. Set the blocks together in rows of 13 as shown in the photo, alternating Block A and Block B. Start odd-numbered rows with Block A and even-numbered rows with Block B. Join the rows.

6. Add border: Seam the 3½" x 44" black print strips as necessary to make strips long enough to border the quilt. See page 108 for information on attaching straight-cut borders.

7. Layer with batting and backing; quilt or tie.

Quilting Suggestion: The quilt shown in the photo is finished with crow footing (page 111). As an alternative, consider quilting diagonal lines along the "chains" formed by the Four-Patch blocks and concentric squares in the areas where the four triangles meet, as shown.

8. Bind with straight or bias strips of fabric.

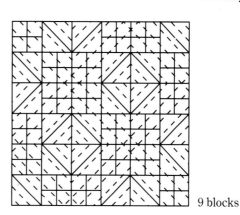

9 blocks

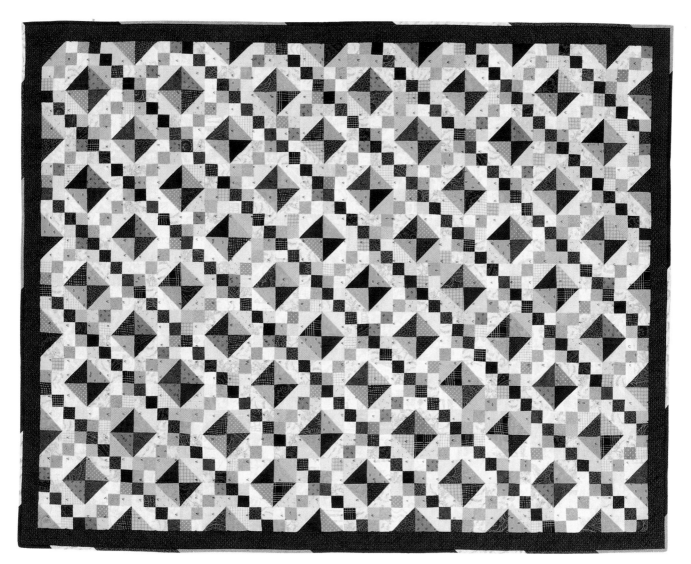

Mysterious Buckeye Beauty by Carol Rhoades, 1991, Anchorage, Alaska, 66" x 84".
This scrappy classic is made from an assortment of red, gray, black, and tan fabrics and is finished
with crow footing and a multi-fabric binding.

Puss in the Corner

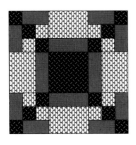

Puss in the Corner
13½" block

Dimensions: 62" x 78"

12 blocks, 13½", set 3 across and 4 down with 3"-wide sashing; 4½"-wide border with corner squares.

Materials: 44"-wide fabric

4 yds. mauve print for blocks, sashing, and border
1⅛ yds. raspberry print for blocks, sashing squares, and corner squares
1⅛ yds. light blue print for blocks
3⅞ yds. fabric for backing
⅝ yd. fabric for 298" of narrow binding
Batting and thread to finish

Cutting: All measurements include ¼" seams.

From the mauve print:

Cut 7 strips, 2" x 44", for blocks.

Cut 6 strips, 3½" x 44", for blocks. Cut 3 of the strips into 48 rectangles, 2" x 3½". *Leave 3 strips uncut.*

From the length of the remaining fabric, cut 2 strips, 5" x 75", and 2 strips, 5" x 68", for border.

From the remaining piece of fabric, cut 31 rectangles, 3½" x 14", for sashing.

From the raspberry print:

Cut 8 strips, 2" x 44", for blocks.

Cut 2 strips, 5" x 44". Cut the strips into 16 squares, 5" x 5", for block centers and corner squares.

Cut 2 strips, 3½" x 44". Cut the strips into 20 squares, 3½" x 3½", for sashing squares.

From the light blue print:

Cut 7 strips, 3½" x 44", for blocks.
Cut 5 strips, 2" x 44", for blocks.

DIRECTIONS

1. Join 5 of the 2" x 44" raspberry strips to the 2" x 44" light blue strips to make 5 strip units as shown. The strip units should measure 3½" wide when sewn. Cut the units into 96 segments, 2" wide, and join the segments into 48 Four Patches.

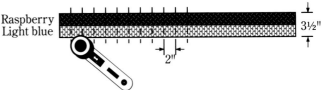

2. Join the 2" x 3½" mauve rectangles to the Four Patches. Make sure the raspberry corners of the Four Patches are oriented as shown.

3. Join the 3 uncut 3½" x 44" mauve strips to the 3 remaining 2" x 44" raspberry strips to make 3 strip units as shown. The units should measure 5" wide when sewn. Cut the units into 48 segments, 2" wide.

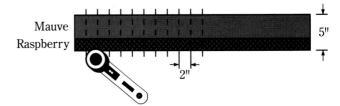

4. Join the segments to the Four-Patch units.

5. Join the 3½" x 44" light blue strips to the 2" x 44" mauve strips to make 7 strip units as shown. The units should measure 5" wide when sewn. Cut the units into 48 segments, 5" wide.

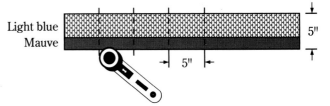

6. Using the units made in steps 4 and 5 and the 5" raspberry squares, piece 12 Puss in the Corner blocks as shown.

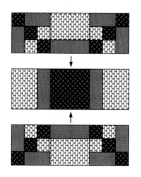

7. Set blocks together with 3½" x 14" mauve sashing pieces and 3½" x 3½" raspberry sashing squares as shown in the photo.

8. Add border: Measure the length and width of the quilt at the center. Cut the 5" x 75" mauve strips to the lengthwise measurement of quilt and join to quilt sides. Cut the 2 remaining strips to the original crosswise measurement of quilt and join the 5" raspberry corner squares to the ends of the strips. Stitch to the quilt top and bottom.

9. Layer with batting and backing; quilt or tie.

Quilting Suggestion: The quilt shown in the photo is machine quilted along the raspberry chains. As an alternative, consider superimposing a circular floral or wreath design over the blocks. Fill the background and border areas with a diagonal grid.

10. Bind with straight or bias strips of fabric.

Judy's Choice by Catherine Shultz, 1991, Anchorage, Alaska, 62" x 78". This mauve and blue Puss in the Corner variation is machine quilted along the raspberry chains.

Jacob's Ladder

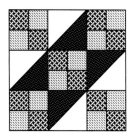

Jacob's Ladder
12" block

Dimensions: 60" x 84"

24 blocks, 12", set 4 across and 6 down; 2"-wide inner border; 1"-wide second border; 3"-wide outer border.

Materials: 44"-wide fabric

1¼ yds. ivory print for blocks and seamed second border

1½ yds. dark gray print for blocks and seamed inner border

1⅛ yds. light gold print for blocks

2 yds. multicolored print (gray, tan, maroon, gold, ivory) for blocks and seamed outer border

3¾ yds. fabric for backing

⅝ yd. fabric for 306" of narrow binding

Batting and thread to finish

Cutting: All measurements include ¼" seams.

From the ivory print:

Cut 6 strips, 4⅞" x 44". Cut the strips into 48 squares, 4⅞" x 4⅞". Cut diagonally into 96 half-square triangles for blocks.

Cut 8 strips, 1½" x 44", for second border.

From the dark gray print:

Cut 6 strips, 4⅞" x 44". Cut the strips into 48 squares, 4⅞" x 4⅞". Cut diagonally into 96 half-square triangles for blocks.

Cut 8 strips, 2½" x 44", for inner border.

From the light gold print:

Cut 15 strips, 2½" x 44", for blocks.

From the multicolored print:

Cut 15 strips, 2½" x 44", for blocks.

Cut 8 strips, 3½" x 44", for outer border.

DIRECTIONS

1. Join the ivory and dark gray half-square triangles into 96 units as shown.

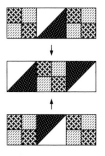

2. Join the 2½" x 44" multicolored and light gold strips to make 15 strip units as shown. The units should measure 4½" wide when sewn. Cut the units into 240 segments, 2½" wide, and join the segments into 120 Four Patches.

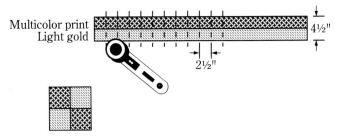

3. Piece 24 Jacob's Ladder blocks as shown.

4. Set the blocks together in rows of 4, rotating every other block so that the small gold squares form a diagonal chain across the surface of the quilt as shown in the photo. Join the rows.

5. Add inner border: Seam the 2½" x 44" dark gray strips as necessary to make strips long enough to border the quilt. See page 108 for information on attaching straight-cut borders.

6. Add second border: Seam the 1½" x 44" ivory strips as necessary. Join to the quilt as for inner border.

7. Add outer border: Seam the 3½" x 44" multicolored print strips as necessary. Measure and join to the quilt as for previous borders.

8. Layer with batting and backing; quilt or tie.

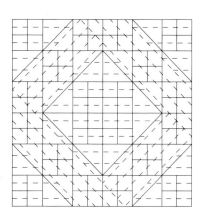

4 blocks

Quilting Suggestion: The quilt shown in the photo was tied. As an alternative, consider quilting diagonal lines along the chains formed by the light gold squares and using straight lines in the other areas as shown.

9. Bind with straight or bias strips of fabric.

Jacob's Ladder by Sheila Rae Robinson, 1990, Palmer, Alaska, 60" x 84". An exotic floral print updates this classic quilt, which is finished by tying.

Independence Ninepatch

Ninepatch A
4½" block

Ninepatch B
4½" block

Dimensions: 48" x 60"

35 Ninepatch blocks, 4½", set on point with plain alternate blocks and "floated" with large corner and side triangles; multiple stripped borders with mitered corners.

Materials: 44"-wide fabric

⅝ yd. assorted dark blue prints for blocks
⅝ yd. assorted white prints for blocks
2 yds. red print for alternate blocks, setting
  triangles, and seamed border
¾ yd. blue print for seamed borders
¾ yd. white print for seamed borders
3 yds. fabric for backing
½ yd. fabric for 234" of narrow binding
Batting and thread to finish

Cutting: All measurements include ¼" seams.

From the dark blue prints:
  Cut 9 strips, 2" x 44", for blocks.

From the white prints:
  Cut 9 strips, 2" x 44", for blocks.

From the red print:
  Cut 8 strips, 4" x 44", for seamed border.
  Cut 3 strips, 5" x 44". Cut the strips into 24
squares, 5" x 5", for alternate blocks.
  Cut 5 squares, 9¾" x 9¾". Cut twice diagonally
into 20 quarter-square triangles for sides.
  Cut 2 squares, 7" x 7". Cut diagonally into 4
half-square triangles for corners.

From the blue print:
  Cut 24 strips, 1" x 44", for seamed border.

From the white print:
  Cut 8 strips, 1½" x 44", for seamed border.
  Cut 8 strips, 1¼" x 44", for seamed border.

DIRECTIONS

1. Join 6 of the 2" x 44" dark blue strips and 3 of the 2" x 44" white strips to make 3 strip units as shown. The units should measure 5" wide when sewn. Cut the units into 52 segments, 2" wide.

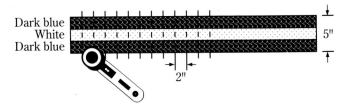

2. Join the remaining 2" x 44" dark blue and white strips to make 3 strip units as shown. The units should measure 5" wide when sewn. Cut the units into 53 segments, 2" wide.

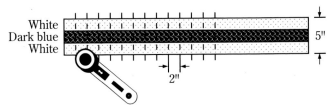

3. Join the segments into 18 Ninepatch Block A and 17 Ninepatch Block B.

4. Set the blocks together in diagonal rows with the red alternate blocks, side, and corner triangles. Join the rows as shown in the photo. The corner and side triangles have been cut large enough to allow the Ninepatch blocks to "float" (page 106); trim and square up the outside edges after the quilt top has been assembled, if needed. To set blocks on point, see "Assembling On-Point Quilts," page 106.

5. Piece borders: Seam the blue and white strips to make pieces long enough to border the quilt. Join the strips into 4 stripped border units as shown, staggering the seams.

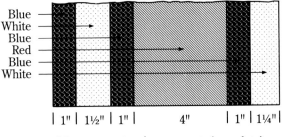

Measurements given are cut sizes of strips.

6. Following the general instructions starting on page 107, measure and stitch the borders to the quilt, mitering the corners.

7. Layer with batting and backing; quilt or tie.

Quilting Suggestion: The quilt shown in the photo was quilted with perle cotton in an allover diagonal grid, with chained hearts from a commercial stencil in the border. (See "Utility Quilting" on page 111.) As an alternative, consider counterbalancing the linear look of the quilt by using a leafy, allover pattern, like Grape Ivy (page 125), run on the diagonal.

8. Bind with straight or bias strips of fabric.

Independence Ninepatch by Judy Hopkins, 1991, Anchorage, Alaska, 48″ x 60″. An abundance of borders frames this simple Ninepatch quilt, which is utility quilted with navy perle cotton.

Ninepatch Strippy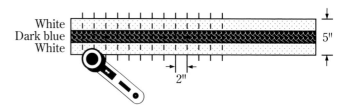

Ninepatch A
4½" block

Ninepatch B
4½" block

Dimensions: 40" x 52"

18 blocks, 4½", set on point in 3 rows of 6; border-stripe sashing strips.

Materials: 44"-wide fabric

⅜ yd. assorted dark blue prints for blocks
⅜ yd. assorted white prints for blocks
1 yd. pink print for setting triangles
1¼ yds. border stripe for sashing strips
1⅝ yds. fabric for backing
½ yd. fabric for 202" of narrow binding
Batting and thread to finish

Cutting: All measurements include ¼" seams.

From the dark blue prints:
   Cut 6 strips, 2" x 44", for blocks.

From the white prints:
   Cut 6 strips, 2" x 44", for blocks.

From the pink print:
   Cut 2 strips, 9¾" x 44". Cut the strips into 8 squares, 9¾" x 9¾". Cut twice diagonally into 32 quarter-square triangles for sides.
   Cut 2 strips, 7" x 44". Cut the strips into 6 squares, 7" x 7". Cut diagonally into 12 half-square triangles for corners.

From the border stripe:
   Cut 4 *lengthwise* strips, about 8" wide, depending on the configuration of the border stripe, for sashing strips.

DIRECTIONS

1. Join 4 of the 2" x 44" dark blue strips and 2 of the 2" x 44" white strips to make 2 strip units as shown. The units should measure 5" wide when sewn. Cut the units into 27 segments, 2" wide.

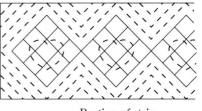

2. Join the remaining 2" x 44" dark blue and white strips to make 2 strip units as shown. The units should measure 5" wide when sewn. Cut the units into 27 segments, 2" wide.

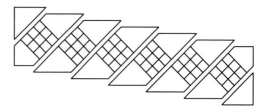

3. Join the segments into 9 Ninepatch Block A and 9 Ninepatch Block B.

4. Set the blocks together in 3 rows with the pink side and corner triangles as shown. The side and corner triangles have been cut large enough to allow the Ninepatch blocks to "float" (page 106); trim the side triangles ½" beyond the points of the Ninepatch blocks to allow ¼" of float on the tops and bottoms of the strips. Trim and square up the corners and ends, if needed; leave more float at the ends of strips.

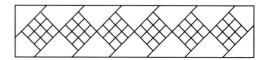

5. Set the rows together with the border-stripe sashing strips as shown in the photo.

6. Layer with batting and backing; quilt or tie.

Quilting Suggestion: In the quilt shown in the photo, hearts have been quilted into the centers of the Ninepatch blocks; the corner triangles were quilted with parallel diagonal lines, and the side triangles with concentric V shapes as shown. The border stripe is completed with

Portion of strip

"squiggles" taken from the Squiggly Stars
pattern (page 120). As an alternative, outline a
dominant shape in the border stripe.

7. Bind with straight or bias strips of fabric.

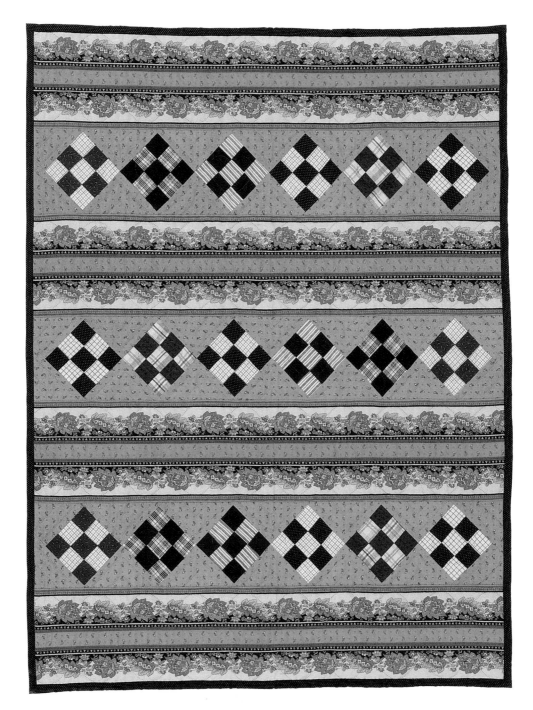

Ninepatch Strip by Judy Hopkins, 1991, Anchorage, Alaska,
40" x 52". This strippy-style quilt features Ninepatch blocks and a
charming, floral border stripe.

Square in a Square

Block A
7¾"

Block B
7¾"

Dimensions: 72" x 94"

83 blocks, 7¾", set on point and "floated" with large setting triangles.

Materials: 44"-wide fabric

1½ yds. assorted light and medium blue prints for blocks
1½ yds. assorted light and medium brown prints for blocks
1½ yds. assorted dark blue prints for blocks
1½ yds. assorted dark brown prints for blocks
2 yds. navy blue print for setting triangles
5⅝ yds. fabric for backing
⅝ yd. fabric for 350" of narrow binding
Batting and thread to finish

Cutting: All measurements include ¼" seams.

From the light and medium blue prints:
Cut 28 squares, 6" x 6", for block centers.
Cut 28 squares, 4¾" x 4¾". Cut diagonally into 56 half-square triangles for block corners.

From the light and medium brown prints:
Cut 27 squares, 6" x 6", for block centers.
Cut 28 squares, 4¾" x 4¾". Cut diagonally into 56 half-square triangles for block corners.

From the dark blue prints:
Cut 14 squares, 6" x 6", for block centers.
Cut 55 squares, 4¾" x 4¾". Cut diagonally into 110 half-square triangles for block corners.

From the dark brown prints:
Cut 14 squares, 6" x 6", for block centers.
Cut 55 squares, 4¾" x 4¾". Cut diagonally into 110 half-square triangles for block corners.

From the navy blue print:
Cut 6 squares, 18" x 18". Cut twice diagonally into 24 quarter-square triangles for sides.
Cut 2 squares, 12½" x 12½". Cut diagonally into 4 half-square triangles for corners.

DIRECTIONS

1. Piece 28 Block A and 55 Block B as shown. Use a single fabric for all the corner pieces in each block.

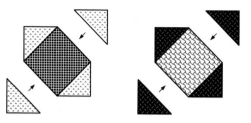

2. Set the blocks together in diagonal rows with the navy blue corner and side triangles; join the rows as shown in the photo. Trim and square up the outside edges after the quilt top has been assembled, if needed. To set blocks on point, see "Assembling On-Point Quilts," page 106.

3. Layer with batting and backing; quilt or tie.

Quilting Suggestion: Quilt with diagonal lines as shown, or consider an allover pattern, such as Hooked on Cables (page 124), run on the diagonal.

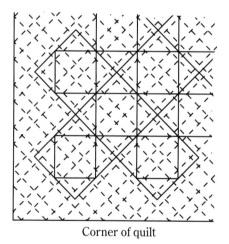

Corner of quilt

4. Bind with straight or bias strips of fabric.

Square within a Square by Jeanie Smith, 1989, Anchorage, Alaska, 72" x 94". Stars appear and disappear in this blue, brown, and purple quilt; the large-scale print used for the binding adds more sparkle. (Collection of Ramona Chinn)

Envelope

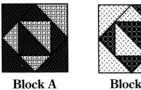

Block A
12"

Block B
12"

Dimensions: 72" x 72"

36 blocks, 12", set 6 across and 6 down; no border.

Materials: 44"-wide fabric

18 light and medium prints (tans, golds, rusts, lavenders, blues) for blocks: ¼ yd. each of 6 fabrics, and a "fat eighth" (9" x 22") each of 12 other fabrics

18 dark prints (browns, reds, purples, blues) for blocks: ¼ yd. each of 12 fabrics and a "fat eighth" (9" x 22") each of 6 other fabrics

4½ yds. fabric for backing

⅝ yd. fabric for 306" of narrow binding

Batting and thread to finish

Cutting: All measurements include ¼" seams.

From *each* of the ¼-yard pieces of fabric:
    Cut 1 square, 7¼" x 7¼". Cut twice diagonally into quarter-square triangles (A).
    Cut 4 squares, 6⅞" x 6⅞". Cut diagonally into half-square triangles (B).

From *each* of the fat eighths of fabric:
    Cut 1 square, 7¼" x 7¼". Cut twice diagonally into quarter-square triangles (A).
    Cut 2 squares, 6⅞" x 6⅞". Cut diagonally into half-square triangles (B).

DIRECTIONS

1. Piece 24 Block A and 12 Block B as shown. Use a single fabric for all of the envelope pieces and a single fabric for all of the background pieces in each block.

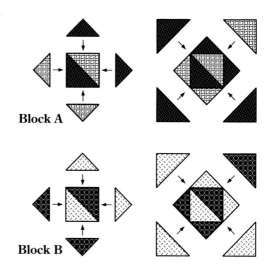

Block A

Block B

2. Set the blocks together in rows of 6, rotating every other block as shown in the photo. Join the rows.

3. Layer with batting and backing; quilt or tie.

Quilting Suggestion: Emphasize the envelope shapes by outline quilting ¼" inside the seams; fill the background area with diagonal lines as shown. As an alternative, consider a distinctive allover pattern like Rhynia (page 126).

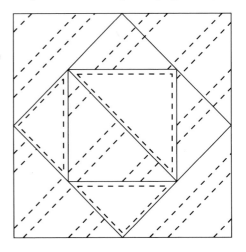

1 block

4. Bind with straight or bias strips of fabric.

Mellow Motion by Ramona Chinn, 1988, Anchorage, Alaska, 72" x 72". This traditional Envelope quilt features rich tans, browns, reds, and purples.

Hayes' Corner Variation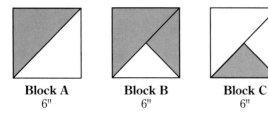

Block A
6"

Block B
6"

Block C
6"

Dimensions: 78" x 96"

99 blocks, 6", set 9 across and 11 down with 3"-wide sashing; no border.

Materials: 44"-wide fabric

2¼ yds. light print for blocks
2 yds. dark blue print for blocks
3¼ yds. light red print for sashing
⅞ yd. medium blue print for sashing squares
5¾ yds. fabric for backing
¾ yd. fabric for 366" of narrow binding
Batting and thread to finish

Cutting: All measurements include ¼" seams.

From the light print:

Cut 9 strips, 6⅞" x 44". Cut the strips into 44 squares, 6⅞" x 6⅞". Cut diagonally into 88 half-square triangles for blocks.

Cut 1 strip, 7¼" x 44". Cut the strip into 5 squares, 7¼" x 7¼". Cut twice diagonally into 20 quarter-square triangles for blocks.

Cut 1 square, 6½" x 6½", for center of quilt.

From the dark blue print:

Cut 9 strips, 6⅞" x 44". Cut the strips into 45 squares, 6⅞" x 6⅞". Cut diagonally into 90 half-square triangles for blocks.

Cut 1 strip, 7¼" x 44". Cut the strip into 5 squares, 7¼" x 7¼". Cut twice diagonally into 20 quarter-square triangles for blocks.

From the light red print:

Cut 17 strips, 6½" x 44", for sashing. Cut 9 of the strips into 98 rectangles, 3½" x 6½". *Leave 8 strips uncut.*

From the medium blue print:

Cut 8 strips, 3½" x 44", for sashing.

DIRECTIONS

1. Using 80 each of the light print and dark blue half-square triangles, piece 80 Block A.

2. Using the remaining half-square triangles and the light print and dark blue quarter-square triangles, piece 10 Block B and 8 Block C.

3. Join 6½" x 44" light red strips and 3½" x 44" medium blue strips to make 8 strip units as shown. The units should measure 9½" wide when sewn. Cut the units into segments, 3½" wide.

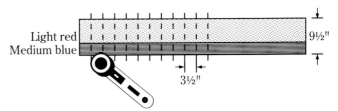

Light red
Medium blue

9½"

3½"

4. Join the segments made in step 3 with 10 of the 3½" x 6½" light red rectangles to make 10 sashing strips as shown. Each sashing strip requires 8 segments and 1 rectangle.

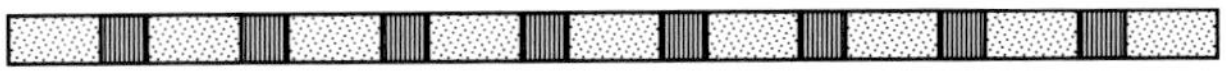

5. Set the blocks together in rows of 9 with the remaining 3½" x 6½" light red rectangles, orienting the light and dark areas of the blocks so that concentric diamond shapes will be formed when the rows are set together as shown in the photo. Join the rows with the sashing strips made in step 4.

6. Layer with batting and backing; quilt or tie.

Quilting Suggestion: Quilt the sashing with straight lines and the blocks with diagonal lines to emphasize the underlying diamond shapes as shown.

Center of quilt

7. Bind with straight or bias strips of fabric.

January 16, 1991 by Ruth E. Horvath, 1991, Wasilla, Alaska, 78" x 96". In this Hayes' Corner variation, a grid of light red and teal floats above the navy and beige diamonds. (Collection of Kathleen Horvath Hall)

Double Pinwheel

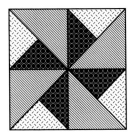

Double Pinwheel
8" block

Dimensions: 68" x 92"

70 blocks, 8", set 7 across and 10 down; 6"-wide border.

Materials: 44"-wide fabric

1½ yds. assorted light prints for background
⅓ yd. each of 10 different medium prints (rusts, browns, blues) for large pinwheels
¼ yd. each of 10 different dark prints (rusts, browns, blues) for small pinwheels
1½ yds. light print for seamed border
5½ yds. fabric for backing
⅝ yd. fabric for 338" of narrow binding
Batting and thread to finish

Cutting: All measurements include ¼" seams.

From the light prints:
   Cut 70 squares, 5¼" x 5¼". Cut twice diagonally into 280 quarter-square triangles for backgrounds.

From *each* of the medium prints:
   Cut 2 strips, 4⅞" x 44". Cut the strips into 14 squares, 4⅞" x 4⅞". When all 10 fabrics have been cut, you will have a total of 140 squares. Cut the squares diagonally into 280 half-square triangles for large pinwheels.

From *each* of the dark prints:
   Cut 1 strip, 5¼" x 44". Cut the strip into 7 squares, 5¼" x 5¼". When all 10 fabrics have been cut, you will have a total of 70 squares. Cut the squares twice diagonally into 280 quarter-square triangles for small pinwheels.

From the light border print:
   Cut 8 strips, 6½" x 44", for seamed border.

DIRECTIONS

1. Piece 70 Double Pinwheel blocks as shown. Use a single fabric for the large pinwheel, a single fabric for the small pinwheel, and a single fabric for the background in each block.

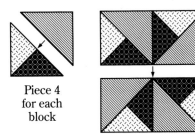

Piece 4
for each
block

2. Set the blocks together in rows of 7 as shown in the photo; join the rows.
3. Add border: Seam the 6½" x 44" light print strips as necessary to make strips long enough to border the quilt. See page 108 for information on attaching straight-cut borders.
4. Layer with batting and backing; quilt or tie.

Quilting Suggestion: Outline quilt the small, dark pinwheels ¼" inside the seams; fill the other areas with diagonal lines as shown. Or, try an allover repeat pattern, like Fandango (page 123), run on the diagonal.

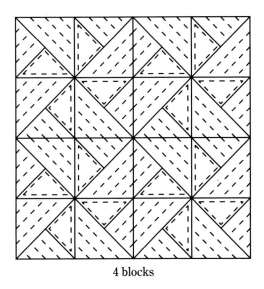

4 blocks

5. Bind with straight or bias strips of fabric.

*Scrappy Pinwheels by Carol Rhoades, 1989, Anchorage, Alaska, 68" x 92". The scrappy Double
Pinwheel blocks include several fabrics from the fifties and sixties.*

Old Favorite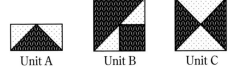

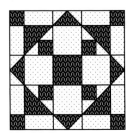

Old Favorite
16" block

Note: In order to eliminate unnecessary seams, this quilt is constructed in units, which are then joined into rows, rather than into blocks.

Dimensions: 60" x 76"

12 blocks, 16", set 3 across and 4 down; 6"-wide border

Materials: 44"-wide fabric

2½ yds. white print for blocks
3¼ yds. dark blue print for blocks and border
3¾ yds. fabric for backing
⅝ yd. fabric for 290" of narrow binding
Batting and thread to finish

Cutting: All measurements include ¼" seams.

From the white print:

Cut 13 strips, 4½" x 44". Cut 2 of the strips into 28 rectangles, 2½" x 4½". Cut the remaining strips into 82 squares, 4½" x 4½".

Cut 5 strips, 2⅞" x 44". Cut the strips into 62 squares, 2⅞" x 2⅞". Cut diagonally into 124 half-square triangles.

Cut 2 strips, 5¼" x 44". Cut the strips into 9 squares, 5¼" x 5¼". Cut twice diagonally into 36 quarter-square triangles.

From the dark blue print:

Cut 3 strips, 4⅞" x 44". Cut the strips into 24 squares, 4⅞" x 4⅞". Cut diagonally into 48 half-square triangles.

Cut 3 strips, 4½" x 44". Cut the strips into 18 squares, 4½" x 4½", and 10 rectangles, 2½" x 4½".

From the *length* of the remaining dark blue print:

Cut 2 strips, 2½" x 84". Cut the strips into 52 squares, 2½" x 2½".

Cut 1 strip, 5¼" x 84". Cut the strip into 12 squares, 5¼" x 5¼". Cut twice diagonally into 48 quarter-square triangles.

Cut 4 strips, 7" x 84", for borders.

DIRECTIONS

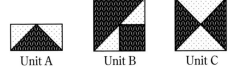

Unit A   Unit B   Unit C

1. Using 14 of the dark blue quarter-square triangles and 28 of the small white half-square triangles, piece 14 Unit A.
2. Using the remaining small, white half-square triangles, 48 of the small, dark blue squares, and the large, dark blue half-square triangles, piece 48 Unit B.
3. Using the remaining dark blue quarter-square triangles and 34 of the white quarter-square triangles, piece 17 Unit C.
4. Using small, dark blue squares, dark blue and white rectangles, and Unit A, make 2 Row A as shown.

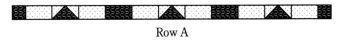

Row A

5. Using large white squares, white rectangles, and Unit B, make 8 Row B as shown.

Row B

6. Using large white and dark blue squares, Unit A, and Unit C, make 4 Row C as shown.

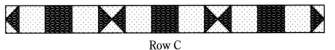

Row C

7. Using the remaining pieces, make 3 Row D as shown.

Row D

8. Join the rows as shown in the full-quilt drawing on page 93. Rows marked * in the drawing are turned upside down.
9. Add borders. (See page 108.)

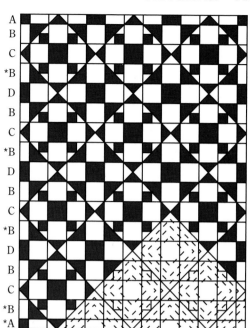

10. Layer with batting and backing; quilt or tie.

Quilting Suggestion: The quilt gives the appearance of being made from two different block patterns, set on point. Emphasize that look by quilting concentric diamonds within each of the two distinct "patterns," or use concentric squares as shown in the photo.

11. Bind with straight or bias strips of fabric.

Northern Nites by Peggy J. Hinchey, 1991, Anchorage Alaska, 60" x 76". This striking two-fabric quilt features blue and white prints and the traditional Old Favorite block.

Attic Window

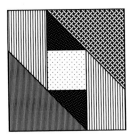

Attic Window
9" block

Dimensions: 58" x 76"

35 blocks, 9", set 5 across and 7 down; ½"-wide inner border, 6"-wide outer border.

Materials: 44"-wide fabric

1½ yds. light blue solid for blocks
⅞ yd. medium blue solid for blocks
¾ yd. dark blue solid for blocks and seamed inner border
½ yd. peach solid for blocks
⅞ yd. lavender solid for blocks
1½ yds. mottled light blue fabric for seamed outer border
3⅝ yds. fabric for backing
⅝ yd. fabric for 286" of narrow binding
Batting and thread to finish

Cutting: All measurements include ¼" seams.

From the light blue solid:
Cut 14 strips, 3½" x 44". Cut the strips into 70 rectangles, 3½" x 6⅞". Nip the lower right-hand corner of each rectangle at a 45° angle as shown.

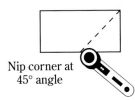

Nip corner at
45° angle

From the medium blue solid:
Cut 4 strips, 6⅞" x 44". Cut the strips into 18 squares, 6⅞" x 6⅞". Cut diagonally into 36 half-square triangles.

From the dark blue solid:
Cut 4 strips, 3⅞" x 44". Cut the strips into 35 squares, 3⅞" x 3⅞". Cut diagonally into 70 half-square triangles.
Cut 8 strips, 1" x 44", for seamed inner border.

From the peach solid:
Cut 4 strips, 3½" x 44". Cut the strips into 35 squares, 3½" x 3½".

From the lavender solid:
Cut 4 strips, 6⅞" x 44". Cut the strips into 18 squares, 6⅞" x 6⅞". Cut diagonally into 36 half-square triangles.

From the mottled light blue fabric:
Cut 8 strips, 6½" x 44", for outer border.

DIRECTIONS

1. Piece 35 Attic Window blocks as shown.

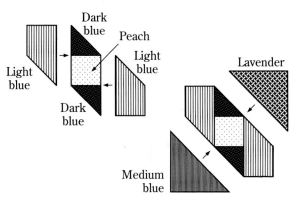

2. Set the blocks together in rows of 5 as shown in the photo; join the rows.
3. Add inner border: Seam the 1" x 44" dark blue strips as necessary to make strips long enough to border the quilt. See page 108 for information on attaching straight-cut borders.
4. Add outer border: Seam the 6½" x 44" mottled, light blue strips as necessary. Measure and join to the quilt as for inner border.
5. Layer with batting and backing; quilt or tie.

Quilting Suggestion: Outline quilt the window ¼" inside the seams; quilt diagonal lines in the large triangles and quilt vertical lines in the remaining portion of the block as shown.

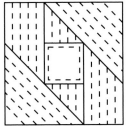

1 block

6. Bind with straight or bias strips of fabric.

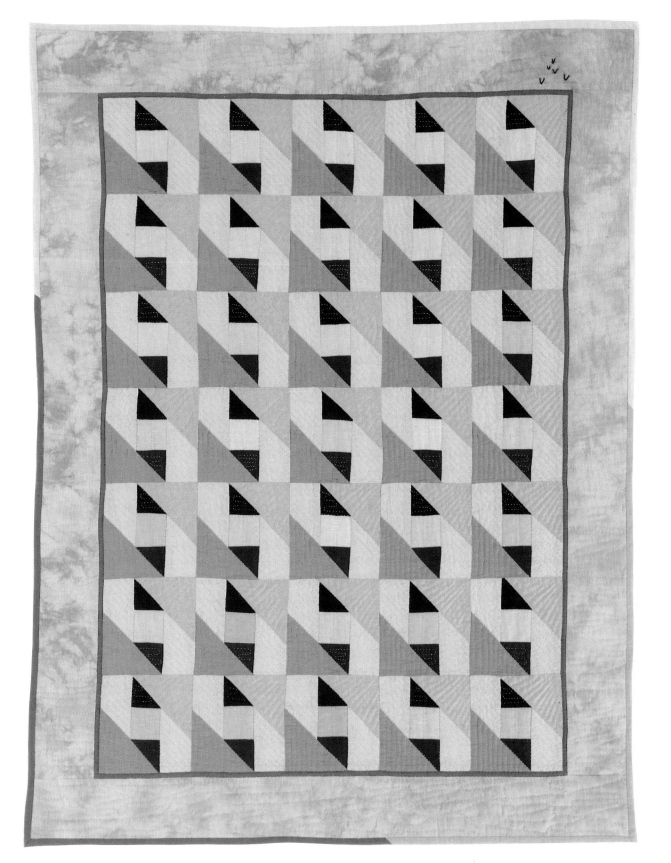

Reflections by Jacquelin Carley, 1991, Anchorage, Alaska, 58" x 76". This traditional Attic Window block may be unfamiliar to many quiltmakers; it's executed in soft lavenders, blues, and peaches and is finished with a multi-fabric binding.

Streak of Lightning

Streak of Lightning
6" x 60"

Dimensions: 60" x 84"

9 horizontal "streaks," 6" x 60", set together with 3"-wide sashing strips; no border.

Materials: 44"-wide fabric

3⅔ yds. multicolored print for background
¼ yd. each of 9 different fabrics for "streaks"
3¾ yds. fabric for backing
⅝ yd. fabric for 306" of narrow binding
Batting and thread to finish

Cutting: All measurements include ¼" seams.

From the multicolored print:

Cut 9 strips, 7¼" x 44". Cut the strips into 43 squares, 7¼" x 7¼". Cut twice diagonally into 172 quarter-square triangles.

From the *length* of the remaining multicolored print:

Cut 10 strips, 3½" x 63", for sashing strips.
Cut 1 strip, 3⅞" x 38". Cut the strip into 9 squares, 3⅞" x 3⅞". Cut diagonally into 18 half-square triangles.

From *each* of the 9 different "streak" fabrics:

Cut 1 strip, 7¼" x 44". Cut 5 squares, 7¼" x 7¼", from the strip; cut twice diagonally into 20 quarter-square triangles.
From the remaining piece of the strip, cut 1 square, 3⅞" x 3⅞". Cut diagonally into 2 half-square triangles.

DIRECTIONS

1. Piece 9 Row A/Row B sets. The shaded dark areas in the drawings represent the streak fabric. In each A/B set, combine a single streak fabric with the multicolored background fabric. Start and end each row with small half-square triangles as shown.

Row A

Row B

2. Join the A/B sets into streaks.
3. Measure the length of the streaks and cut the 10 multicolored sashing strips to that length.
4. Set the streaks together, adding a sashing strip between each streak and at the top and bottom of the quilt as shown in the photo.
5. Layer with batting and backing; quilt or tie.

Quilting Suggestion: Emphasize the "streaks" with zigzag quilting; continue the zigzags into the background, or use a different quilting design in the multicolored areas as shown.

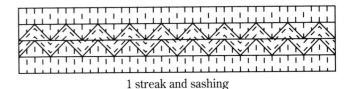

1 streak and sashing

6. Bind with straight or bias strips of fabric.

Hot Flashes by Ella Bosse, 1991, Anchorage, Alaska, 60″ x 84″. Contemporary, fluorescent fabrics bring the traditional Streak of Lightning pattern into the nineties.

Ribbon Quilt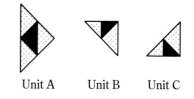

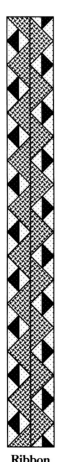

Dimensions: 42" x 54"

7 vertical "ribbons," 6" x 54"; no border.

Note: Bias squares are not used in this quilt, although it might appear logical to use them at first glance. Bias squares, if used, would have to be cut to an unusual size—2.62". A standard cutting size is possible with the quarter-square triangles required, and straight grain is maintained on the outside edges of the ribbons.

Materials: 44"-wide fabric

1½ yds. pink print for background
1½ yds. dusty rose print for "ribbons"
⅔ yd. maroon print for small accent
    triangles
2¾ yds. fabric for backing
½ yd. fabric for 210" of narrow binding
Batting and thread to finish

Cutting: All measurements include ¼" seams.

Ribbon
54" x 6"

From the pink print:
    Cut 11 strips, 4¼" x 44". Cut the strips into 93 squares, 4¼" x 4¼". Cut twice diagonally into 372 quarter-square triangles.
    Cut 1 strip, 2⅜" x 44". Cut the strip into 7 squares, 2⅜" x 2⅜". Cut diagonally into 14 half-square triangles.

From the dusty rose print:
    Cut 6 strips, 7¼" x 44". Cut the strips into 30 squares, 7¼" x 7¼". Cut twice diagonally into 120 quarter-square triangles.
    Cut 1 strip, 3⅞" x 44". Cut the strip into 7 squares, 3⅞" x 3⅞". Cut diagonally into 14 half-square triangles.

From the maroon print:
    Cut 4 strips, 4¼" x 44". Cut the strips into 30 squares, 4¼" x 4¼". Cut twice diagonally into 120 quarter-square triangles.
    Cut 1 strip, 2⅜" x 44". Cut the strip into 7 squares, 2⅜" x 2⅜". Cut diagonally into 14 half-square triangles.

Directions

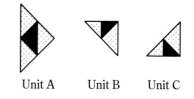

Unit A   Unit B   Unit C

1. Using pink and maroon quarter-square triangles, piece 119 Unit A.
2. Using remaining pink and maroon quarter-square triangles and small pink and maroon half-square triangles, piece 7 Unit B and 7 Unit C.
3. Join the pieced units with the dusty rose triangles to make 7 Row A and 7 Row B. Start and end Row A with a dusty rose half-square triangle; start and end Row B with Units B and C
4. Join the rows, alternating A and B.
5. Layer with batting and backing; quilt or tie.

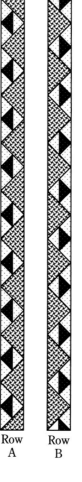

Row   Row
A   B

Quilting Suggestion: Emphasize the lines of the quilt by following the zigzag lines as shown.

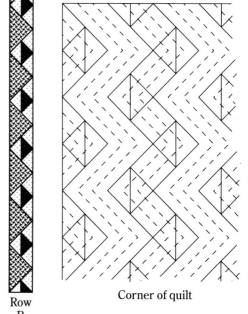

Corner of quilt

6. Bind with straight or bias strips of fabric.

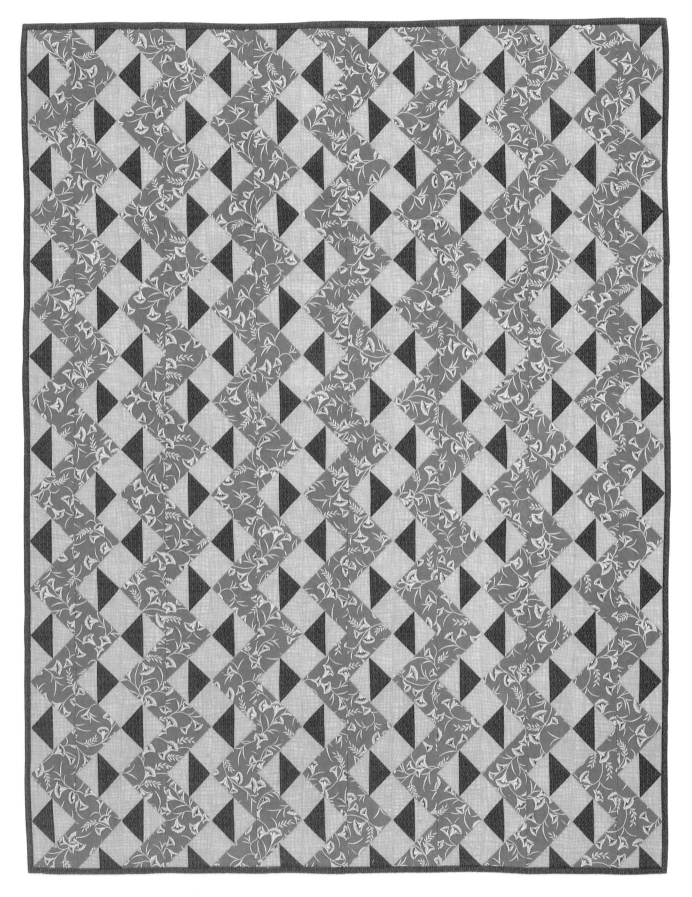

Cathy's Quilt by George Taylor, 1991, Anchorage, Alaska, 42″ x 54″. A Streak of Lightning with a difference, this quilt is based on the traditional Ribbon Block. (Collection of Catherine Shultz)

Blackford's Beauty

Blackford's Beauty
12" block

Dimensions: 73½" x 87½"

20 blocks, 12", set 4 across and 5 down with 2"-wide sashing; ¾"-wide inner border; 3"-wide second border; 4"-wide outer border.

Materials: 44"-wide fabric

4⅛ yds. light print for background and seamed second border

1¼ yds. medium blue print for blocks, sashing squares, and seamed inner border

2¼ yds. dark blue print for blocks and seamed outer border

5¼ yds. fabric for backing

⅝ yd. fabric for 340" of narrow binding

Batting and thread to finish

Cutting: All measurements include ¼" seams.

From the light print:

Cut 8 strips, 2" x 44", for blocks.

Cut 10 strips, 3½" x 44", for blocks. Cut 2 of the strips into 20 squares, 3½" x 3½". Cut 4 of the strips into 80 rectangles, 2" x 3½". *Leave 4 strips uncut.*

Cut 3 strips, 4¼" x 44". Cut the strips into 20 squares, 4¼" x 4¼". Cut twice diagonally into 80 quarter-square triangles for blocks.

Cut 5 strips, 2⅜" x 44". Cut the strips into 80 squares, 2⅜" x 2⅜". Cut diagonally into 160 half-square triangles for blocks.

Cut 17 strips, 2½" x 44". Cut the strips into 49 rectangles, 2½" x 12½", for sashing.

Cut 8 strips, 3½" x 44", for seamed second border.

From the medium blue print:

Cut 12 strips, 2" x 44", for blocks.

Cut 2 strips, 2½" x 44". Cut the strips into 30 squares, 2½" x 2½", for sashing squares.

Cut 8 strips, 1¼" x 44", for seamed inner border.

From the dark blue print:

Cut 3 strips, 4¼" x 44". Cut the strips into 20 squares, 4¼" x 4¼". Cut twice diagonally into 80 quarter-square triangles for blocks.

Cut 5 strips, 2⅜" x 44". Cut the strips into 80 squares, 2⅜" x 2⅜". Cut diagonally into 160 half-square triangles for blocks.

Cut 4 strips, 3½" x 44". Cut the strips into 80 rectangles, 2" x 3½", for blocks.

Cut 8 strips, 4½" x 44", for seamed outer border.

DIRECTIONS

1. Join the 2" x 44" light print strips and 8 of the 2" x 44" medium blue strips to make 8 strip units as shown. The units should measure 3½" wide when sewn. Cut the units into 160 segments, 2" wide, and join segments into 80 Four Patches.

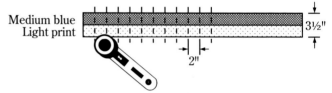

2. Join the 2" x 3½" light print rectangles to the Four Patches. Make sure the medium blue corners of the Four Patches are oriented as shown in the drawing.

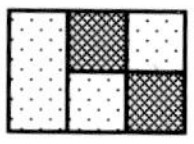

3. Join the uncut 3½" x 44" light print strips to the remaining 2" x 44" medium blue strips to make 4 strip units as shown. The units should measure 5" wide when sewn. Cut the units into 80 segments, 2" wide.

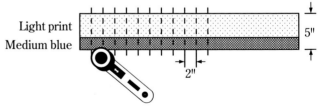

4. Join the segments to the Four-Patch units to make 80 Unit A as shown.

Unit A

Blackford's Beauty by Roxanne Carter, 1990, Edmonds, Washington, 73½" x 87½". The pastel color scheme is enhanced by the chain of blue squares across the quilt top.

5. Using the light print and dark blue half- and quarter-square triangles, piece 80 Unit B and 80 Unit C as shown.

Unit B　　　Unit C

6. Join Units B and C with the dark blue rectangles to make 80 Unit D as shown.

Unit D

7. Join Units A and D and light print squares to make 20 Blackford's Beauty blocks as shown.

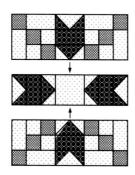

8. Set the blocks together with the light print sashing pieces and the medium blue sashing squares as shown in the photo. The medium blue squares will form a "chain" across the surface of the quilt.
9. Add inner border: Seam the 1¼" x 44" medium blue strips as necessary to make strips long enough to border the quilt. See page 108 for information on attaching straight-cut borders.

10. Add second border: Seam the 3½" x 44" light print strips as necessary. Measure and join to the quilt as for inner border.
11. Add outer border: Seam the 4½" x 44" dark blue strips as necessary. Measure and join to the quilt as for previous borders.
12. Layer with batting and backing; quilt or tie.

Quilting Suggestion: Outline quilt the center star shape and the dark blue points. Fill the background area with diagonal lines as shown.

1 block

13. Bind with straight or bias strips of fabric.

Finishing Your Quilt

This section begins with basic information on squaring up blocks and joining them in either straight or on-point (diagonal) sets, and continues with an in-depth discussion of other finishing techniques: borders; marking the quilting lines; backings and batting; layering the quilt; quilting and tying; bindings; and sleeves and labels. A variety of finishing approaches have been used in the quilts included in this book; the photos are an excellent source of ideas.

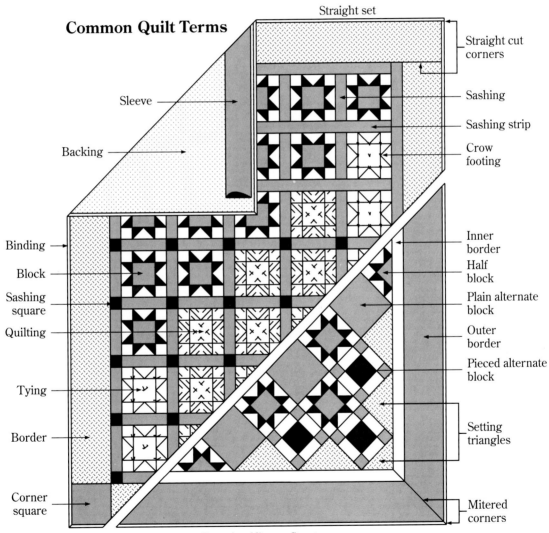

Common Quilt Terms

Straight set

Straight cut corners

Sleeve

Sashing

Backing

Sashing strip

Crow footing

Binding

Inner border

Block

Half block

Sashing square

Plain alternate block

Quilting

Outer border

Pieced alternate block

Tying

Setting triangles

Border

Corner square

Mitered corners

On-point (diagonal) set

SQUARING UP BLOCKS

Some quiltmakers find it necessary to trim or square up their blocks before they assemble them into a quilt top. If you trim, be sure to leave ¼" seam allowances beyond any points or other important block details that fall at the outside edges of the block.

To square up blocks, Anchorage quilter Jackie Carley suggests cutting a piece of plastic-coated freezer paper to the proper size (finished block size plus seam allowance); iron the freezer paper to your ironing board cover, plastic side down. Pin the block edges to the edges of the freezer-paper guide and gently steam press; allow the blocks to cool before you unpin and remove them.

STRAIGHT SETS

In straight sets, blocks are laid out in rows that are parallel to the edges of the quilt. Constructing a straight-set quilt is simple and straightforward. When blocks are to be set side by side without sashing, simply stitch them together in rows; then, join the rows to complete the patterned section of the quilt. If alternate blocks are used, cut or piece them to the same size as the primary blocks (including seam allowances), then lay out the primary and alternate blocks in checkerboard fashion and stitch the rows.

When setting blocks together with plain sashing, cut the vertical sashing pieces to the same length as the blocks (including seam allowances) and to whatever width you have determined is appropriate. Join the sashing pieces and the blocks to form rows, starting and ending each row with a block. Then, join the rows with long strips of the sashing fabric, cut to the same width as the shorter sashing pieces. Make sure that the corners of the blocks are aligned when you stitch the rows together. Add the left- and right-hand side sashing strips last.

If your sashing includes corner squares of a different color or fabric than the rest of the sashing (sashing squares), cut the vertical sashing pieces and join them to the blocks to form rows, starting and ending each row with a sashing piece. Cut the horizontal sashing pieces to the same size as the vertical pieces. Cut sashing squares to the same dimensions as the width of the sashing pieces and join them to the horizontal sashing pieces to make sashing strips, starting and ending each row with a

sashing square. Join the rows of blocks with these pieced sashing strips.

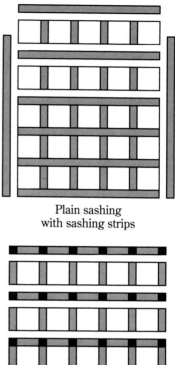

Plain sashing
with sashing strips

Sashing with
sashing squares

ON-POINT SETS

Quilts that are set on point are constructed in diagonal rows, with half- and quarter-blocks or setting triangles added to complete the sides and corners of the quilt. If you are designing your own quilt and have no photo or assembly diagram for reference, sketch the quilt on a piece of graph paper so you can see how the rows will go together and how many setting pieces you will need.

Plain setting triangles can be quick-cut from squares. You will always need four corner triangles; to maintain straight grain on the outside edges of the quilt, these should be half-square triangles. Two squares cut to the proper dimensions and divided once on the diagonal will yield four half-square triangles needed for corners.

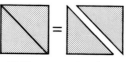

Half-square triangles
for corners

Check your quilt sketch to see how many side triangles will be needed. To maintain straight grain on the outside edges, the side triangles should be quarter-square triangles. A square cut to the proper dimensions and divided twice on the diagonal will yield four quarter-square triangles, so you will need to divide the total number of triangles needed by four, round up to the next whole number, and cut and divide that many squares.

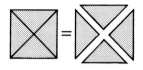

Quarter-square
triangles for sides

How do you determine the "proper dimensions" for cutting these squares? The calculations are based on the finished size of the blocks, and they vary, depending on whether the blocks are set side by side or are separated by sashing. Though you can use common mathematical formulas to calculate the cutting dimensions down to a gnat's eyebrow (and the formulas have been included at the end of this section for you math whizzes), I prefer the "cut 'em big and trim 'em down" method, which requires mostly simple addition and just one tedious calculation.

The Tedious Calculation is this: Multiply the finished size of your block by 1.414 to find the *finished diagonal measurement* of the block. You will need this measurement during the planning stage in order to determine the overall size of the patterned section of an on-point quilt and, later, to calculate the cutting dimensions for setting triangles. If the prospect of translating the result of this calculation from decimals to inches is unnerving, just multiply the finished size of your block by 1.5 to get the *approximate finished diagonal measurement* of the block. The result will be accurate enough for the "cut 'em big" approach to setting triangles.

For on-point sets where the blocks are set side by side with no sashing, determine the proper dimensions to cut the squares as follows:

Corners: Add 2½" to the finished measurement of the block. Cut two squares to that size; cut the squares once on the diagonal.
Sides: Calculate the approximate finished diagonal measurement of the block (finished block size x 1.5); add 3" to the result. Cut squares to that

size; cut the squares twice on the diagonal. Each square yields four triangles.

For on-point sets where the blocks are separated by sashing, determine the proper dimensions to cut the squares as follows:

Corners: Multiply the finished width of the sashing by 2; add the result to the finished size of the block, then add 2½". Cut two squares to that size; cut the squares once on the diagonal.
Sides: Add the finished width of the sashing to the finished size of the block. Calculate the approximate finished diagonal measurement (block + sash x 1.5); add 3". Cut squares to that size; cut the squares twice on the diagonal. Each square yields four triangles.

These somewhat slapdash calculations will work just fine; exact numbers are unnecessary. If you ever need to know how to calculate cutting dimensions for setting triangles with utter precision, here are the gnat's eyebrow formulas I mentioned above. First, some basic geometry:

When you know the length of the side of a square or right triangle, multiply by 1.414 to get the diagonal measurement.

When you know the length of the diagonal of a square or right triangle, divide by 1.414 to get the side measurement.

For on-point sets where the blocks are set side by side, with no sashing, determine the proper dimensions to cut the squares as follows:

Corners: Divide the finished block size by 1.414. Add .875 (for seams). Round the result up to the nearest ⅛". (Decimal-to-inch conversions are given on page 106.) Cut two squares to that size; cut the squares once on the diagonal.
Sides: Multiply the finished block size by 1.414. Add 1.25 (for seams). Round the result up to the nearest ⅛". Cut squares to that size; cut the squares twice on the diagonal. Each square yields four triangles.

For on-point sets where the blocks are separated by sashing, determine the proper dimensions to cut the squares as follows:

Corners: Multiply the finished width of the sashing by 2. Add the finished block size. Divide the result by 1.414, add .875 (for seams), and round up to the nearest ⅛". (Decimal-to-inch conversions are given below.) Cut two squares to that size; cut the squares once on the diagonal.
Sides: Add the finished width of the sashing to the finished size of the block. Multiply the result by 1.414, add 1.25 (for seams), and round up to the nearest ⅛". Cut squares to that size; cut the squares twice on the diagonal. Each square yields four triangles.

Decimal-to-Inch Conversions

.125	= ⅛"	.625	= ⅝"
.25	= ¼"	.75	= ¾"
.375	= ⅜"	.875	= ⅞"
.50	= ½"		

ASSEMBLING ON-POINT QUILTS

As mentioned in the previous section, quilts laid out with the blocks set on point are constructed in diagonal rows. To avoid confusion, lay out all the blocks and setting pieces in the proper configuration before you start sewing. In an on-point set where blocks are set side by side without sashing, simply pick up and sew one row at a time; then, join the rows.

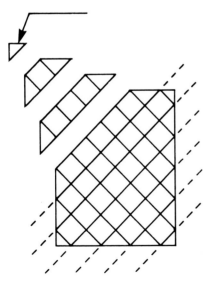

Assembly Diagram for On-Point Set

When you use the "cut 'em big" approach for the setting triangles, the side and corner triangles will be larger than the blocks. Align the square corners of the triangle and the block when you join the side triangles to the blocks, leaving the excess at the "point" end of the setting triangle.

Stitch and press the seam, then trim the excess even with the edge of the block. Attach the corner triangles last, centering the triangles on the blocks so that any excess or shortfall is distributed equally on each side.

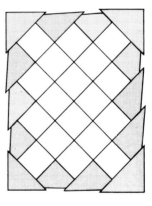

Side: Align square corners of block and triangle; stitch. Trim after pressing.

When sewn, your quilt top will look something like this:

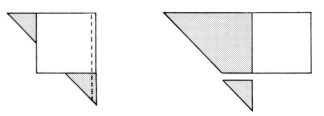

Obviously, some trimming and squaring up will be needed. At this point, you can make a decision about whether to leave some excess fabric so the blocks will "float" or to trim the setting triangles so that only a ¼" seam allowance remains. Use the outside corners of the blocks to align your cutting guide and trim as desired; make sure the corners are square.

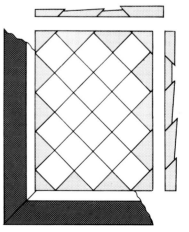

Trimming to leave ¼" seam allowance. Border, when added, will come to the corners of the blocks.

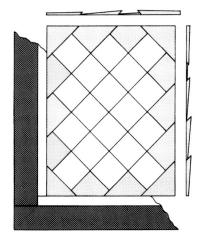

Trimming to allow blocks to "float"

The assembly order for on-point sets that include sashing is a little more complex. You can see from the drawing below that the side setting triangles span a block plus one piece of the sashing, and the corner triangles span a block plus two sashing pieces. Before laying out your blocks, sashing pieces, and setting triangles in preparation for sewing, make a photocopy or tracing of your paper quilt plan and slice it into diagonal rows so you can see exactly which pieces constitute a particular row. Once you have joined the pieces into rows, start joining the rows from the bottom right corner and work toward the center. When you reach the center, set that piece aside and go to the top left corner, again working toward the center. Add the top right and bottom left corner triangles last, after the two main sections have been joined.

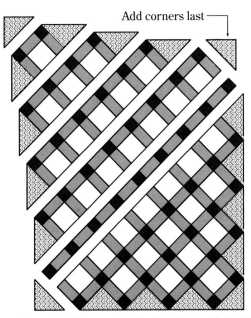

Add corners last

Assembly Diagram for On-Point Set with Sashing

Some of us have difficulty getting on-point quilts to lie flat. You can minimize potential problems by taking a few precautions during the cutting and assembly process. Make sure that the individual blocks are absolutely square and are all the same size. Plain or pieced alternate blocks should be perfectly square and exactly the same size as the primary blocks. The 90° corners of the side setting triangles should be truly square. Since these triangles are quick-cut on the bias, sometimes the corners are not square; it's worth taking the time to double-check. When you join blocks to setting triangles, feed them into the sewing machine with the block, which has a straight-grain edge on top and the bias-edged setting triangle on the bottom.

BORDERS

Whether to add a border to your quilt or not is entirely up to you. Some quilts seem to resist borders. If you have tried several different bordering options and none seems to work, perhaps the piece wants to be finished without a border at all or with a border on only one or two sides. Many quilts will happily accept a "1-2-3" border—an inner border, a second border, and an outer border in 1:2:3 proportions (1" inner, 2" second, and 3" outer borders or 1½" inner, 3" second, and 4½" outer borders, for example).

Though many of us avoid adding elaborately pieced borders to our quilts because of the additional work involved, some quilts demand them. As an alternative, try a multi-fabric border: Use a different fabric on each edge of the quilt; use one fabric for the top and right edges and a different fabric for the bottom and left edges; or, join random chunks of several different fabrics until you have pieces long enough to form borders. Quiltmakers who buy fabric in small cuts often resort to multi-fabric borders out of necessity, as they rarely have enough of any one fabric to border an entire quilt!

Because extra yardage is required to cut borders on the lengthwise grain, plain border strips commonly are cut along the crosswise grain and seamed when extra length is needed. These seams should be pressed open for minimum visibility. To assure a flat, square quilt, cut border strips extra long and trim the strips to the proper length after the actual dimensions of the patterned center section of the quilt are known.

Most of the quilts in the pattern section of this

book are completed with borders that have straight-cut corners; a few may have borders with mitered corners.

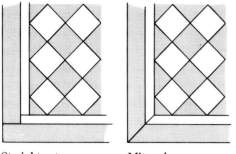

Straight-cut corners   Mitered corners

To make a border with straight-cut corners, measure the length of the patterned section of the quilt at the center, from raw edge to raw edge. Cut two border strips to that measurement and join them to the sides of the quilt with a ¼" seam, matching the ends and centers and easing the edges to fit. Then, measure the width of the quilt at the center from edge to edge, including the border pieces that you just added. Cut two border strips to that measurement and join them to the top and bottom of the quilt, matching ends and centers and easing as necessary.

 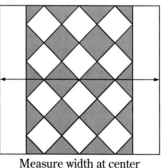

Measure length   Measure width at center
at center   after adding side borders

Note: Do not measure the outer edges of the quilt! Often, these edges measure longer than the quilt center due to stretching during construction; the edges might even be two different lengths. To keep the finished quilt as straight and square as possible, you must measure the centers.

To make mitered corners, first estimate the finished outside dimensions of your quilt *including borders*. Border strips should be cut to this length plus at least ½" for seam allowances; it's safer to add 2"–3" to give yourself some leeway. If your quilt is to have multiple borders, sew the individual strips together and treat the resulting unit as a single piece for mitering.

Mark the centers of the quilt edges and the centers of the border strips. Stitch the borders to the quilt with a ¼" seam, matching the centers; the border strip should extend the same distance at each end of the quilt. Start and stop your stitching ¼" from the corners of the quilt; press the seams toward the borders.

Lay the first corner to be mitered on the ironing board, pinning as necessary to keep the quilt from pulling and the corner from slipping. Fold one of the border units under, at a 45° angle. Work with the fold until seams or stripes meet properly; pin at the fold, then check to see that the outside corner is square and that there is no extra fullness at the edges. When everything is straight and square, press the fold.

Starting at the outside edge of the quilt, center a piece of 1" masking tape over the mitered fold; remove pins as you apply the tape.

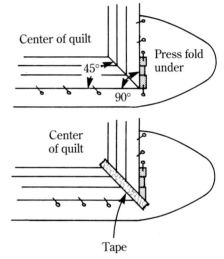

Tape

Unpin the quilt from the ironing board and turn it over. Fold the center section of the quilt diagonally from the corner, right sides together, and align the long edges of the border strips. Draw a light pencil line on the crease created when you pressed the fold. Stitch on the pencil line, then remove the tape; trim the excess fabric and press the seam open. Repeat these steps for the remaining three corners.

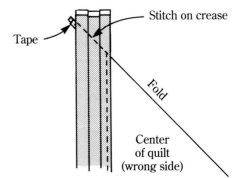

MARKING THE QUILTING LINES

Marking may not be necessary if you are planning to quilt "in the ditch" or to outline quilt a uniform distance from seam lines. Some quiltmakers do outline quilting "by eye," though many others use ¼" masking tape to mark these lines as they stitch. You can use masking or drafting tape to mark any straight-line quilting design; simple shapes can be cut from Con-Tact® paper. Apply the tape or adhesive-paper shape when you are ready to quilt and remove promptly after you have quilted along its edge; adhesives left on the quilt for any length of time may leave a residue that is difficult to remove.

More complex quilting designs should be marked on the quilt top *before* the quilt is layered with batting and backing. A gridded transparent ruler is useful for measuring and marking straight lines and filler grids. Quilting patterns from books or magazines or hand-drawn designs can be placed underneath the quilt and traced onto the fabric if the quilt fabrics are fairly light; use a light box or put your work against a window if you have difficulty seeing the design.

If you cannot see through the quilt fabric, the design will have to be drawn directly onto the quilt top. Use a precut plastic stencil, or make your own by drawing or tracing the quilting design on clear plastic; cut out the lines with a double-bladed craft knife, leaving "bridges" every inch or two so the stencil will hold its shape. Or, trace the design onto plain paper (or make a photocopy); cover the paper with one or two layers of clear Con-Tact® paper and cut out the lines. You can put small pieces of double-stick tape on the back of the stencil to keep it in place as you mark the lines.

When marking quilting lines, work on a hard, smooth surface. Use a hard lead pencil (number 3 or 4) on light fabrics; for dark fabrics, try a fine-line chalk marker or a silver, nonphoto blue, or white pencil. Ideally, marking lines will remain visible for the duration of the quilting process and can be removed easily when the quilting is done. Light lines are always easier to remove than heavy ones; test to make sure that the markings will wash out after the quilting is completed.

If you are using an allover quilting pattern that does not relate directly to the seams or to a design element of the quilt, you may find it easier to mark the quilting lines on the backing fabric and quilt from the back rather than the front of the quilt.

BACKINGS AND BATTING

Quilt backings should be cut at least 4" wider and 4" longer than the quilt top. A length of 44"-wide fabric will be adequate to back a quilt that is no wider than 40". For a larger quilt, buy extra-wide, dress-weight cotton or sew two or more pieces of fabric together. Use a single fabric, seamed as necessary, to make a backing of adequate size, or piece a simple multi-fabric back that complements the front of the quilt. Early quiltmakers often made pieced backings as a matter of necessity; modern quiltmakers see quilt backings as another place to experiment with color and design.

If you opt for a seamed or pieced backing, trim off selvages before you stitch and press seams open. Seam single-fabric backings horizontally to conserve fabric.

Batting comes packaged in standard bed sizes; it also can be purchased by the yard. Several weights or thicknesses are available. Thick battings are fine for tied quilts and comforters; choose a thinner batting if you intend to quilt by hand or machine.

Thin batting is available in 100% cotton, 100% polyester, and an 80%-20% cotton-polyester blend. The cotton-polyester blend is said to combine the best features of the two fibers. All-cotton batting is soft and drapeable but requires close quilting and produces quilts that are rather flat. Though many quilters like the antique look, some find cotton batting difficult to "needle." Glazed or bonded polyester batting is sturdy, easy to work with, and washes well. It requires less quilting than cotton and has more loft. However, polyester fibers sometimes migrate through fabric, creating tiny white "beards" on the surface of a quilt. The dark gray polyester battings now available are expected to ease this problem for quiltmakers who like to work with dark fabrics; bearding, if it occurs, will be less noticeable.

Unroll your batting and let it relax overnight before you layer your quilt. Some battings may need to be prewashed, while others should definitely *not* be prewashed; be sure to check the manufacturer's instructions.

LAYERING THE QUILT

Once your quilt top has been marked, your backing pieced and pressed, and your batting "relaxed," you are ready to layer the quilt. Spread the backing, wrong side up, on a flat, clean surface; anchor it with pins or masking tape. Spread the batting over the backing, smoothing out any wrinkles; then, center the quilt top on the backing, right side up. Be careful not to stretch or distort any of the layers as you work. Starting in the middle, pin-baste the three layers together, gently smoothing any fullness to the sides and corners.

Now, baste the three layers together with a long needle and light-colored thread; start in the center and work diagonally to each corner, making a large X. Continue basting, laying in a grid of horizontal and vertical lines 6"–8" apart. Finish by basting around the outside edges.

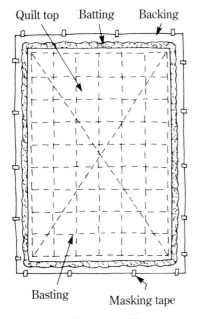

Quilt top   Batting   Backing

Basting   Masking tape

QUILTING AND TYING TECHNIQUES

The purpose of quilting or tying is to keep the three layers together and to prevent the batting from lumping or shifting. Quilts typically are tied, with knots either on the front or the back, or they are machine or hand quilted. Quiet exploration is taking place in this facet of quiltmaking. While several old methods for tying and quilting are being revived, some quiltmakers are stretching tradition by "tying" with eyelets or decorative studs, or quilting with unusual materials, including narrow ribbon, wire, and even cassette tape.

Machine Quilting

Machine quilting is suitable for all types of quilts, from baby and bed quilts that will be washed frequently to glamorous pieces for the wall. With machine quilting, you can quickly complete quilts that might otherwise languish on shelves. The technique provides some creative challenges as well.

Unless you plan to stitch "in the ditch," mark the quilting lines *before* you layer the quilt. Consider using a simple allover grid or a continuous-line quilting design. Basting for machine quilting is often done with safety pins; if you have a large work surface to support the quilt and an even-feed foot for your sewing machine, you should have no problem with shifting layers or untidy pleats, tucks, and bubbles on the back side. Remove the safety pins as you sew. Pull thread ends to the back and work them into the quilt for a more professional look. Try machine quilting with threads of unusual types and weights or experiment with the decorative stitch or twin-needle capabilities of your sewing machine. Double-needle quilting produces an interesting, corded effect. Anchorage quiltmaker Rosie Huntemann uses a technique she calls "bumper-car quilting": Leaving the quilt top unmarked, she stitches along in a casual, free-form manner; when she comes to a safety pin, she veers off in a different direction.

Traditional Hand Quilting

To quilt by hand, you will need short, sturdy needles (called "Betweens"), quilting thread, and a thimble to fit the middle finger of your sewing hand. Most quilters also use a frame or hoop to support their work. Quilting needles run from size 3 to 12; the higher the number, the smaller the needle. Use the smallest needle you can comfortably handle; the smaller the needle, the smaller your stitches will be.

Thread your needle with a single strand of quilting thread about 18" long; make a small knot and insert the needle in the top layer about 1" from the place where you want to start stitching. Pull the needle out at the point where quilting will begin and gently pull the thread until the knot pops through the fabric and into the batting. Begin your quilting line with a backstitch, inserting the needle straight down through all three layers. Proceed by taking small, even running stitches, rocking the needle up and down through all the layers until you have three or four stitches on the needle. Place your other hand underneath the quilt so you can feel the needle point with the tip of your finger when a stitch is taken.

To end a line of quilting, make a small knot close to the last stitch; then, backstitch, running the thread a needle's length through the batting. Gently pull the thread until the knot pops into the batting; clip the thread at the quilt's surface. Remove basting stitches as you quilt, leaving only those that go around the outside edges of quilt.

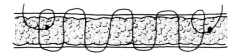

Starting and ending the quilting thread

Utility Quilting

Utility quilting is faster than traditional hand quilting, but "homier" than machine quilting; you use big needles and heavy threads (like perle cotton, several strands of embroidery floss, or Knit-Cro-Sheen™) and take big stitches, anywhere from ⅛" to ¼" in length. The method is well worth considering for casual, scrappy quilts and for pieces you might otherwise plan to machine quilt. Quilts finished with this technique are unquestionably sturdy, and the added surface texture is very pleasing.

You can do utility quilting "freehand," without marking the quilt top, or mark quilting lines as usual. Use the shortest, finest, sharp-pointed needle you can get the thread through; try several different kinds to find the needle that works best for you. I like working with #8 perle cotton and a

#6 Between needle. Keep your stitches as straight and even as possible.

Crow Footing and Other Tacking Techniques

I have an old comforter in my collection that is tied with a technique called "crow footing." Crow footing is done with a long needle and thick thread, such as a single or double strand of perle cotton or Knit-Cro-Sheen™. Isolated fly stitches are worked in a grid across the surface of the quilt; there are no visible knots or dangling threads.

Put your work in a hoop or frame. Use a long, sharp-pointed needle—try cotton darners, millinery needles, or soft-sculpture needles. Make a small knot in the thread and insert the needle in the top layer of the quilt about 1" from A. Pull the needle out at A and gently pull the thread until the knot pops through the fabric and into the batting. Hold the thread down with the thumb and insert the needle at B as shown; go through all three layers and bring the needle out at C. Insert the needle at D and travel through the top layer only to start the next stitch at A. Work in rows from the top to the bottom or from the right to the left of the quilt, spacing the stitches about 2" apart. This leaves a small diagonal stitch on the back of the quilt. To end stitching, bring the needle out at C and make a small knot about ⅛" from the surface of the quilt. Make a backstitch at D, running the thread through the batting an inch or so; pop the knot into the batting and clip the thread at the surface of the quilt.

Crow Footing

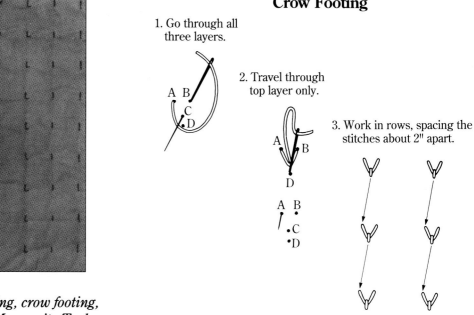

1. Go through all three layers.

2. Travel through top layer only.

3. Work in rows, spacing the stitches about 2" apart.

Row 1   Row 2

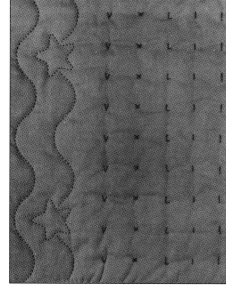

From left to right: Utility quilting, crow footing, cross-stitch, buttonhole stitch, Mennonite Tack, Methodist Knot.

You can substitute a cross-stitch for the isolated fly stitch. Bring the needle out at A. The B-C stitch goes through all three layers; the D-A stitch travels through the top layer only. This leaves a small horizontal stitch on the back of the quilt.

Cross-stitch

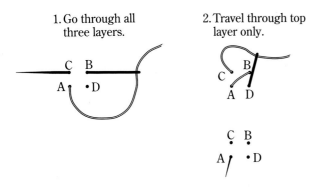

Or, try using an isolated buttonhole stitch. Bring the needle out at A. The B-C stitch goes through all three layers; the D-A stitch travels through the top layer only. This leaves a small horizontal stitch on the back of the quilt.

Buttonhole Stitch

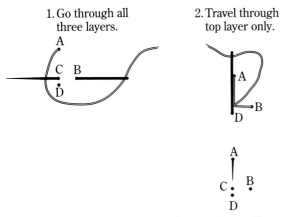

Backstitch tacking is another option. There are two different approaches—the Mennonite Tack and the Methodist Knot. Both stitches are best worked from the right to the left rather than from the top to the bottom of the quilt; they leave a small horizontal stitch on the back of the quilt.

To do the Mennonite Tack, bring the needle out at A and take a backstitch about ¼" long through all three layers, coming back up just a few threads from the starting point (B-C). Reinsert the needle at D and travel through the top layer only to start the next stitch. The tiny second stitch, which should be almost invisible, crosses over the backstitch and locks the tacking.

Mennonite Tack

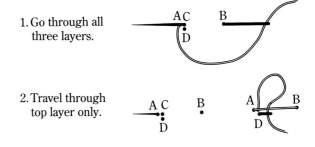

3. Work in rows from right to left.

The Methodist Knot is done with two back-stitches. Bring the needle out at A and take a backstitch through all three layers, coming back up beyond the starting point (B-C). Reinsert the needle at A and travel through the top layer only to start the next stitch.

Methodist Knot

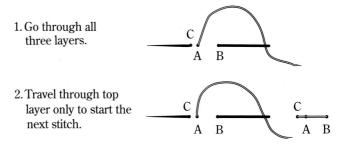

Any of these tacking stitches can be laid in at random, rather than on a uniform grid. Early quiltmakers who used these techniques often worked with the quilt stretched on a large floor frame, rolling in the edges of the quilt as the rows of tacking were completed, thus eliminating the need for basting. Small quilts can be tied or tacked without basting if the layers are spread smoothly over a table or other large, flat work surface.

BINDINGS

When the tying or quilting is complete, prepare for binding by removing any remaining basting threads, except for the stitches around the outside edge of the quilt. Trim the batting and backing even with the edge of the quilt top. Use a rotary cutter and ruler to get accurate, straight edges; make sure the corners are square.

Make enough binding to go around the perimeter of the quilt, plus about 18". The general instructions below are based on ⅜" (finished), double-fold binding, made from strips cut 2½" wide and stitched to the outside edges of the quilt with a ⅜" seam. Cutting dimensions and seam widths for bindings in other sizes are given in the shaded box on page 115.

Straight-grain binding is fine for most applications. Simply cut strips from the lengthwise or crosswise grain of the fabric; one crosswise strip will yield about 40" of binding. For ⅜" (finished) binding, cut the strips 2½" wide. Trim the ends of the strips at a 45° angle and seam the ends to make a long, continuous strip; press seams open. Fold the strip in half lengthwise, wrong sides together, and press.

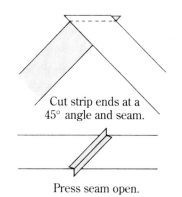

Cut strip ends at a 45° angle and seam.

Press seam open.

Use bias binding if your quilt edge has curves or if you expect the quilt to get heavy use; binding cut on the bias does wear longer. Some quilters cut bias strips from a flat piece of fabric, joining the strips after cutting; others prefer the tubular method for making a continuous bias strip.

To make flat-cut binding, lay out a length of fabric. (Fabric requirements are given below.) Make a bias cut, starting at one corner of the fabric; use the 45° marking on a long cutting ruler as a guide. Then, cut bias strips, measuring from the edges of the initial bias cut. For ⅜"-wide (finished) binding, cut the strips 2½" wide. Seam the ends to make a long, continuous strip; press seams open. Fold the strip in half lengthwise, wrong sides together, and press.

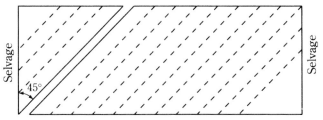

Flat-cut Bias Binding

For ⅜"-wide (finished) binding made from 2½"-wide strips:

¼ yard fabric yields about 125" of binding
⅜ yard fabric yields about 200" of binding
½ yard fabric yields about 275" of binding
⅝ yard fabric yields about 350" of binding
¾ yard fabric yields about 440" of binding

Continuous bias binding can be made from a square of fabric. To determine what size square will yield the amount of bias binding you need, multiply the length of bias needed (in inches) by the width you plan to cut it, then use a pocket calculator to find the square root of the result.

Let's say you are planning to finish a 72" x 84" quilt with ⅜"-wide finished binding, which requires 2½"-wide strips. You will need 330" of binding (quilt perimeter plus 18"); 330 x 2½ = 825. The square root of 825 is 28.72. Thus, a 29"–30" square will yield the 330" of binding you need.

Remove the selvage and mark the top and bottom of the square with pins. Divide the square on the diagonal to yield two half-square triangles.

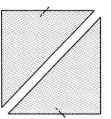

Mark top and bottom of square and divide it on the diagonal.

With right sides together, join the marked sides of the triangles with a ¼" seam; press seam open.

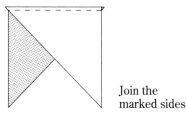

Join the marked sides

Measure and draw lines the width of the binding strips on the wrong side of the fabric, starting at one of the long, bias edges as shown in the drawing at the top of page 114. If the distance between the last line and the bottom edge is less than the strip width needed, trim to the line above. Slice along the top and bottom lines (at the ends closest to the seam) for a distance of about 6", as shown.

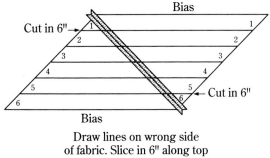

Draw lines on wrong side
of fabric. Slice in 6" along top
and bottom lines.

With right sides together *and the edges offset by the width of one line*, stitch the ends together to form a cylinder; press seam open. Starting at the top, cut along the marked lines to form a continuous bias strip. Fold the strip in half lengthwise, wrong sides together, and press.

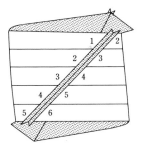

Stitch ends together to form
a cylinder, offsetting edges
by width of one line.

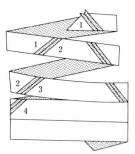

Cut along lines to form
a continuous strip

Two different methods of applying the binding to the quilt are described below. One produces a binding with mitered corners, with the binding applied in a continuous strip around the edges of the quilt. In the second method, measured lengths of binding are applied separately to each edge of the quilt. In both cases, the instructions given are based on ⅜"-wide finished binding; you will need to use a different seam width if your finished binding is narrower or wider than ⅜".

Bindings with Mitered Corners

For a binding with mitered corners, start near the center of one side of the quilt. Place the binding on the front of the quilt, lining up the raw edges of the binding with the raw edges of the quilt. Using an even-feed foot, sew the binding to the quilt with a ⅜"-wide seam; leave the first few inches of the binding loose so that you can join or overlap the beginning and ending of the binding strip later. Be careful not to stretch the quilt or the binding as you sew. When you reach the corner, stop the stitching ⅜" from the edge of the quilt and backstitch; clip threads.

Turn the quilt to prepare for sewing along the next edge. Fold the binding up and away from the quilt; then, fold it again to bring it along the edge of the quilt. There will be an angled fold at the corner; the straight fold should be even with the top edge of the quilt.

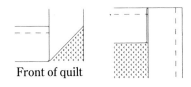

Front of quilt

Stitch from the straight fold in the binding to the next corner, pinning as necessary to keep the binding lined up with the raw edge of the quilt. When you reach the next corner, stop the stitching ⅜" from the edge of the quilt and backstitch; clip threads. Fold the binding as you did at the last corner and continue around the edge of the quilt. When you reach the starting point, fold one end of the binding at a 45° angle; overlap the fold with the other end of the binding and finish stitching.

Fold the binding to the back, over the raw edges of the quilt; the folded edge of the binding should just cover the machine stitching line. Blindstitch the binding in place, making sure your stitches do not go through to the front of the quilt. At the corners, fold the binding to form miters on the front and back of the quilt; stitch down the folds in the miters.

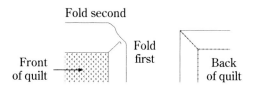

Fold second

Front
of quilt

Fold
first

Back
of quilt

Binding with Measured Strips

Use this binding method if the outside edges of your quilt need to be eased to the binding so that their finished measurements conform to the quilt's center measurements. Straight-grain binding strips work best for this type of binding.

Bind the long edges of the quilt first. Measure the length of the quilt at the center, raw edge to raw edge.

Note: Do not measure the outer edges of the quilt! Often the edges measure longer than the quilt center due to stretching during construction; the edges might even be two different lengths.

From your long strip of binding, cut two pieces of binding to the lengthwise center measurement. Working from the right side of the quilt, pin the binding strips to the long edges of the quilt, matching the ends and centers and easing the edges to fit as necessary. Using an even-feed foot, sew the binding to the quilt with a ⅜"-wide seam. Fold the binding to the back, over the raw edges of the quilt; the folded edge of the binding should just cover the machine-stitching line. Blindstitch the binding in place, making sure your stitches do not go through to the front of the quilt.

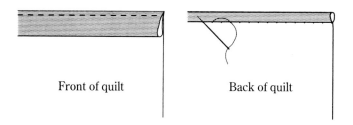

Front of quilt   Back of quilt

Now prepare and sew the binding strips for the shorter edges of the quilt. Measure the width of the quilt at the center, outside edge to outside edge; from the remainder of your long binding strip, cut two pieces to that measurement plus 1". Pin these measured binding strips to the short edges of the quilt, matching the centers and leaving ½" of the binding extending at each end; ease the edges to fit as necessary. Sew the binding to the quilt with a ⅜" seam.

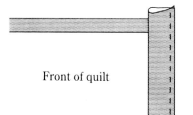

Front of quilt

To finish, fold the extended portion of the binding strips down over the bound edges; then, bring the binding to the back and blindstitch in place as before.

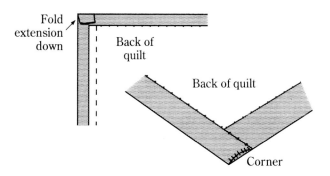

Fold extension down

Back of quilt

Back of quilt

Corner

Strip and seam widths for double-fold bindings in various finished sizes are as follows:

Binding	Strip Width	Seam
¼"	1¾"	¼"
⅜"	2½"	⅜"
½"	3¼"	½"
⅝"	4"	⅝"
¾"	4¾"	¾"

Sleeves and Labels

Quilts that will be displayed on walls should have a sleeve, tacked to the back near the top edge, to hold a hanging rod. I put sleeves on all my quilts, even those intended for beds, so they can be safely hung if they are suddenly requested for an exhibit or if their owners decide to use them for decoration rather than as bedding.

Sleeves should be a generous width. Use a piece of fabric 6"–8" wide and 1"–2" shorter than the finished width of the quilt at the top edge. Hem the ends. Then, fold the fabric strip in half lengthwise, *wrong* sides together; seam the long, raw edges together with a ¼" seam. Fold the tube so that the seam is centered on one side and press the seam open.

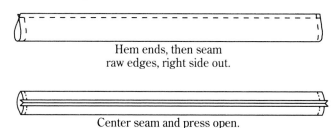

Hem ends, then seam raw edges, right side out.

Center seam and press open.

Place the tube on the back side of the quilt, just under the top binding, with the seamed side against the quilt. Hand sew the top edge of the sleeve to the quilt, taking care not to catch the front of the quilt as you stitch.

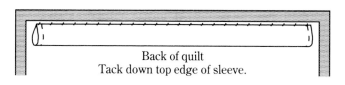

Back of quilt
Tack down top edge of sleeve.

Push the front side of the tube up so the top edge covers about half of the binding (providing a little "give" so the hanging rod does not put strain on the quilt itself) and sew the bottom edge of the sleeve in place, as shown below.

Slide a curtain rod, a wooden dowel, or a piece of lath through the sleeve. The seamed side of the sleeve will keep the rod from coming into direct contact with the quilt. Suspend the rod on brackets. Or, attach screw eyes or drill holes at each end of the rod and slip the holes or eyes over small nails.

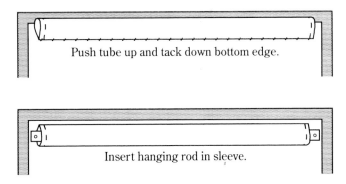

Push tube up and tack down bottom edge.

Insert hanging rod in sleeve.

Be sure to sign and date your work! At the very least, embroider your name and the year the quilt was completed on the front or back of the quilt. Quilt historians and the future owners of your quilts will be interested to know more than just the "who" and "when." Consider tacking a handwritten or typed label to the back of the quilt that includes the name of the quilt, your name, your city and state, the date, who the quilt was made for and why, and any other interesting or important information about the quilt.

Press a piece of plastic-coated freezer paper to the wrong side of the label fabric to stabilize it while you write or type. For a handwritten label, use a permanent marking pen; a multistrike ribbon should be used for typewritten labels. Always test to be absolutely sure the ink is permanent!

Note: Hand- or typewritten labels that safely pass the washing-machine test sometimes run and bleed when they are dry-cleaned.

Repeat Quilting Designs

Allover and repeat quilting patterns have a unifying effect on busy, multi-fabric quilts. Most of us have used allover quilting from time to time, either as background for more elaborate motifs or as the sole pattern for a quilt. The simplest and most familiar allover pattern is the grid, often arranged on the diagonal to form a repeating diamond shape. Other popular, allover patterns include clamshells, basket weave, and concentric circles or arcs.

When any design is repeated in an organized way, a repeat pattern results. The designs, or "repeats," may be isolated shapes, repeated within the boundaries of either a visible or implied grid. When you select a simple heart pattern and draw that heart in the center of every square of a simple one-patch quilt, you are producing an "isolated-design" repeat.

Other repeat designs are organized so that when you trace the design, move the stencil, and trace the design again, a continuous pattern is formed; the design elements are somehow linked or connected. A familiar example is the border pattern or stencil that can be used to draw a continuous cable or vine design. These patterns form a continuous design when you place them end to end; when you place them side by side, the design elements do not connect. I call these two-way repeat patterns. Two-way repeats, though most commonly used in border areas, can also be used in close horizontal, vertical, or diagonal rows to create allover designs across the quilt surface.

Quilting books and magazines occasionally include repeat quilting designs, and a number of repeat patterns are available commercially as stencils. Eight original, two-way repeat patterns have been included here. They are shown on the next two pages in reduced size so you can get an idea of their overall effect when used in repeats. Full-size patterns for each design begin on page 120. If you wish, enlarge or reduce the designs before transferring the pattern to your quilt.

To use the designs, make a stencil according to the instructions given in "Marking the Quilting Lines" (page 109). Include the registration marks (the corner and side crosses) as part of the stencil; mark the "A" and "B" ends with a permanent pen. Draw the pattern, end to end, in a horizontal, vertical, or diagonal row across your quilt, matching registration marks to properly align the design. Always place the "A" end of the pattern against the "B" end to make the pattern repeat properly. Draw a second row adjacent to the first, again matching registration marks. Repeat until pattern covers the entire quilt surface.

The small drawings on pages 118 and 119 show how the patterns look when repeated. Some are most effective when repeated in a half-drop format (a bricklike arrangement), using the midpoint registration marks as a guide for placement of the alternate rows. Or, try treating "A" as the top of the pattern for the first row and as the bottom of the pattern for the second row, alternating across the surface of the quilt.

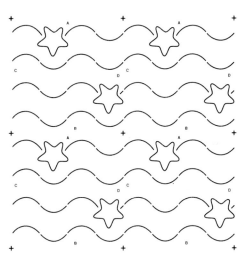

Squiggly Stars in Repeat

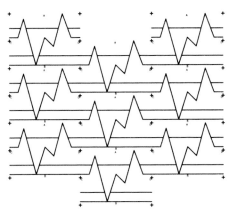

Stock Market in Repeat

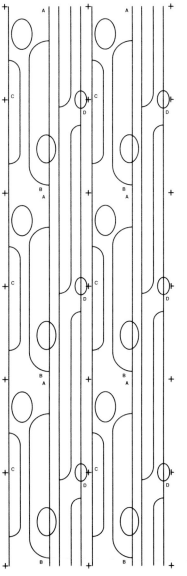

Detroit Deco in Repeat

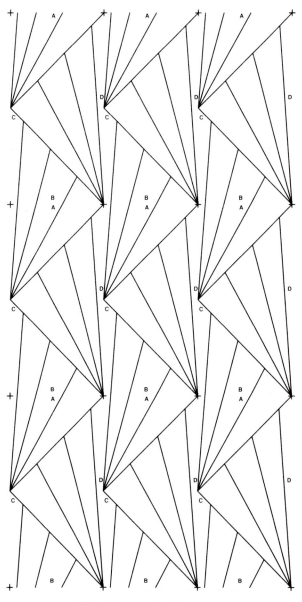

Fandango in Repeat

Hooked on Cables in Repeat

Grape Ivy in Repeat

Rhynia in Repeat

Filigree in Repeat

Squiggly Stars
©1990 Judy D. Hopkins

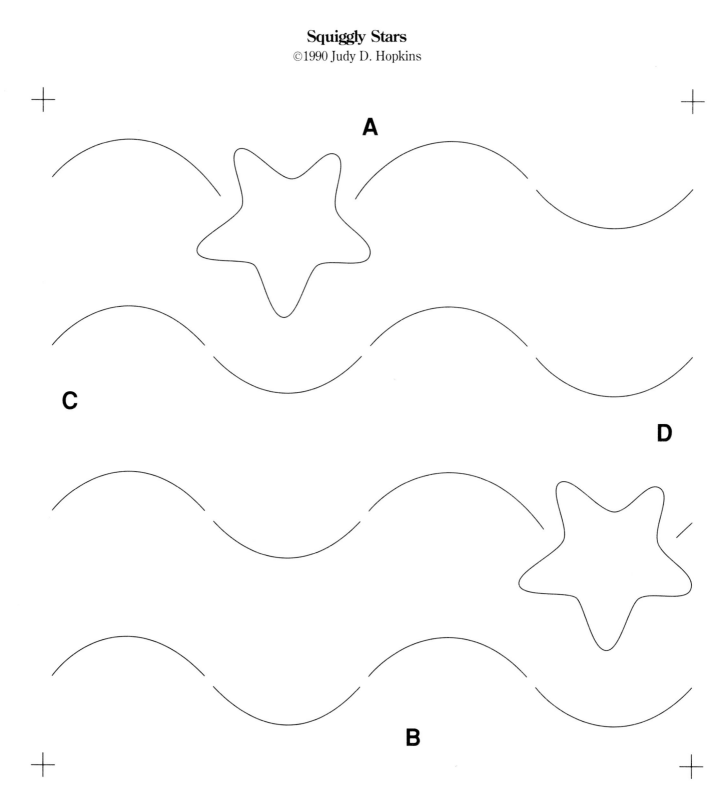

This simple design is especially effective in diagonal rows. Try
marking it on the quilt backing rather than the quilt top;
quilt from the back.

Stock Market
©1991 Judy D. Hopkins

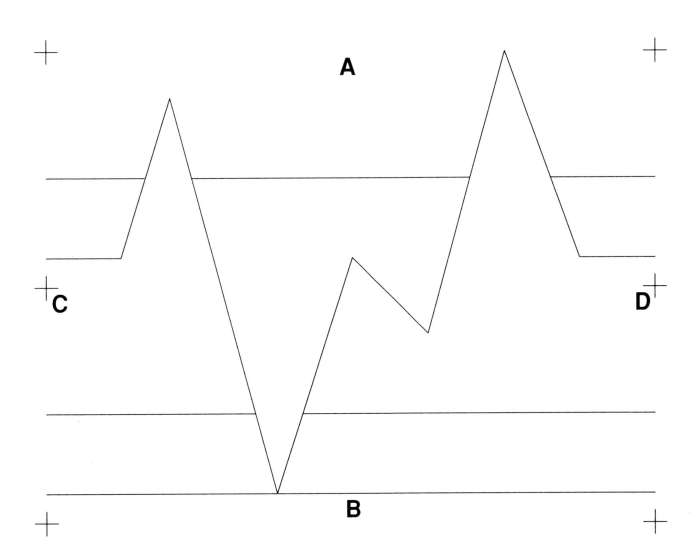

This spiky design must be half-dropped to repeat properly. Use the mid-point registration marks as a guide for placement of the alternate rows, as shown in the repeat sketch.

Detroit Deco
©1989 Judy D. Hopkins

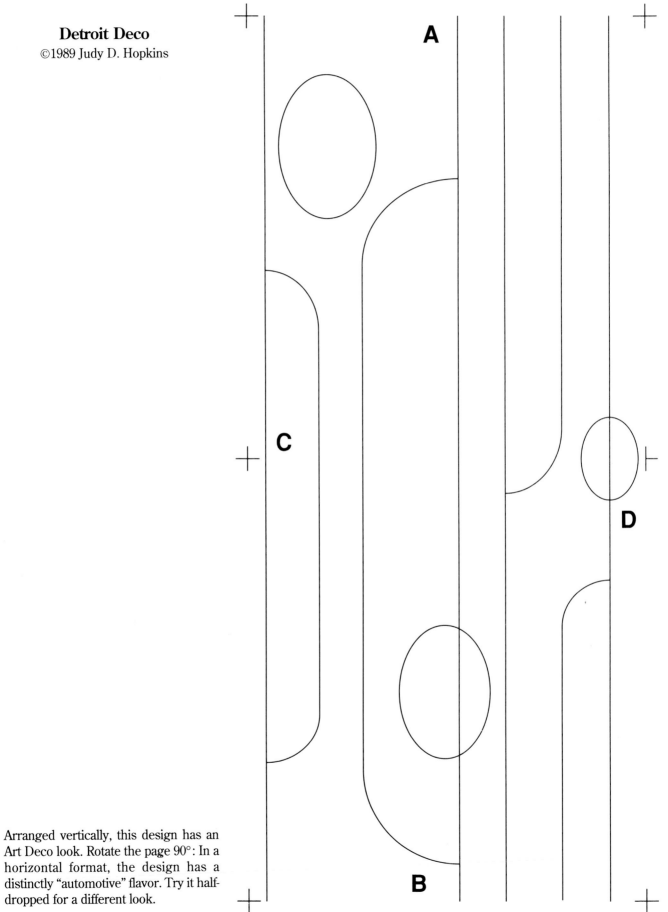

Arranged vertically, this design has an Art Deco look. Rotate the page 90°: In a horizontal format, the design has a distinctly "automotive" flavor. Try it half-dropped for a different look.

Fandango
©1991 Judy D. Hopkins

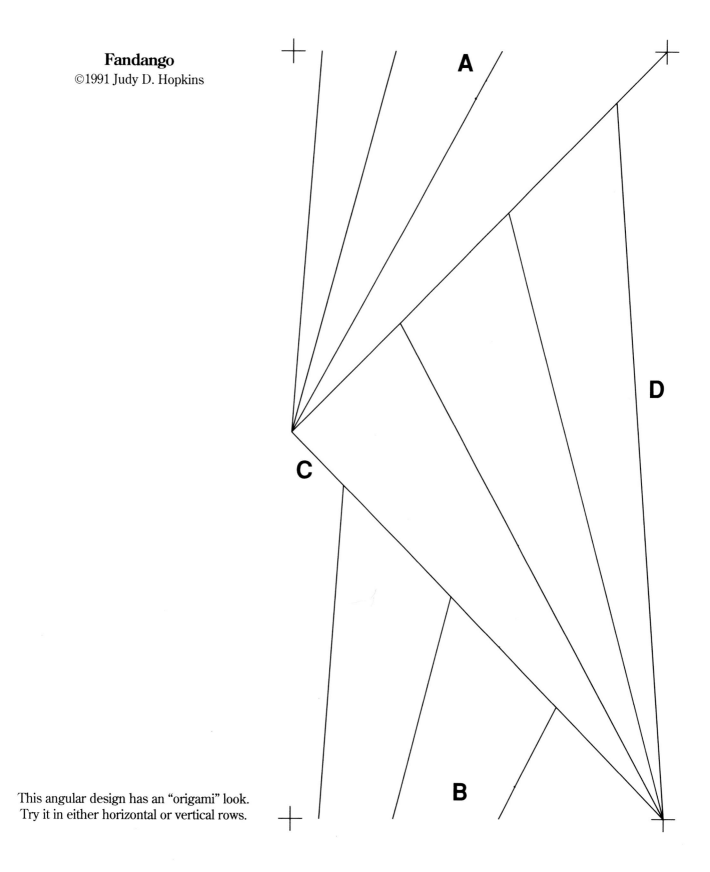

A

B

C

D

This angular design has an "origami" look.
Try it in either horizontal or vertical rows.

Hooked on Cables
©1991 Judy D. Hopkins

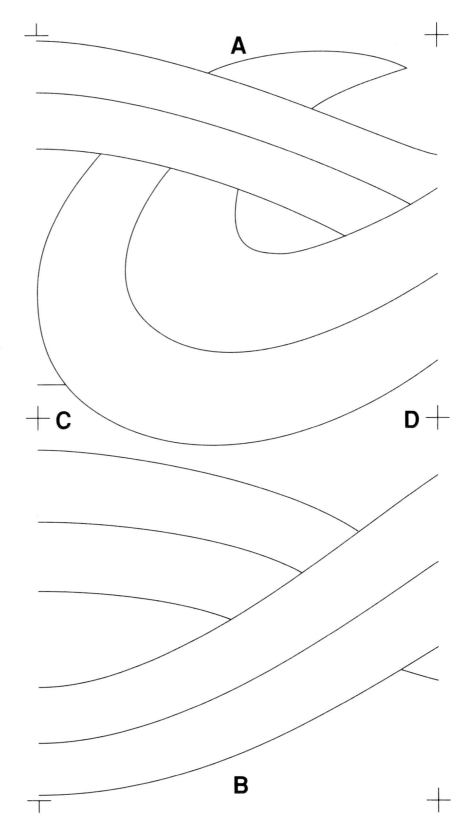

Here's a cable with a twist. Treat "A" as the top of the pattern for the first row, as the bottom of the pattern for the second row, and so on, alternating across the surface of the quilt.

Grape Ivy
©1989 Judy D. Hopkins

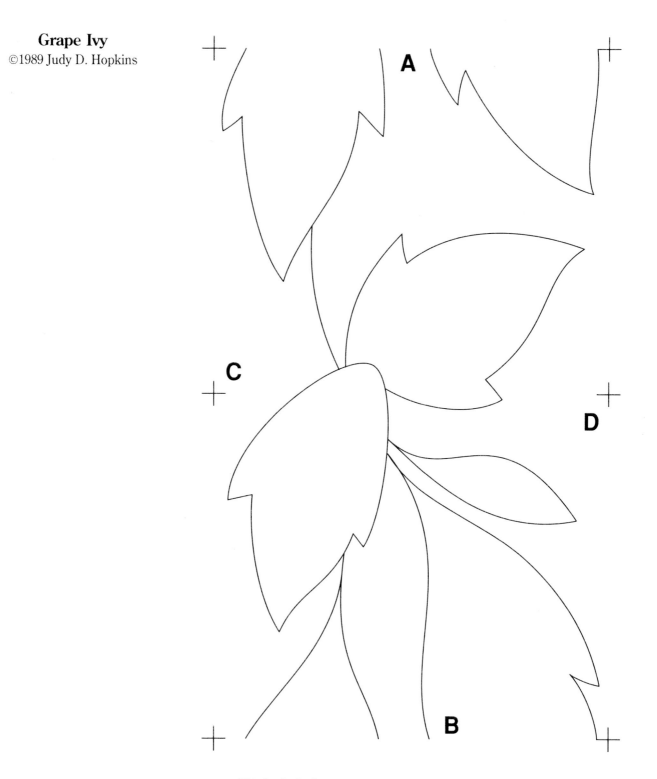

This leafy design repeats most effectively when "A" is treated as the top of the pattern for the first row, as the bottom of the pattern for the second row, and so on, alternating across the surface of the quilt. Try running it in diagonal rows.

Rhynia
©1988 Judy D. Hopkins

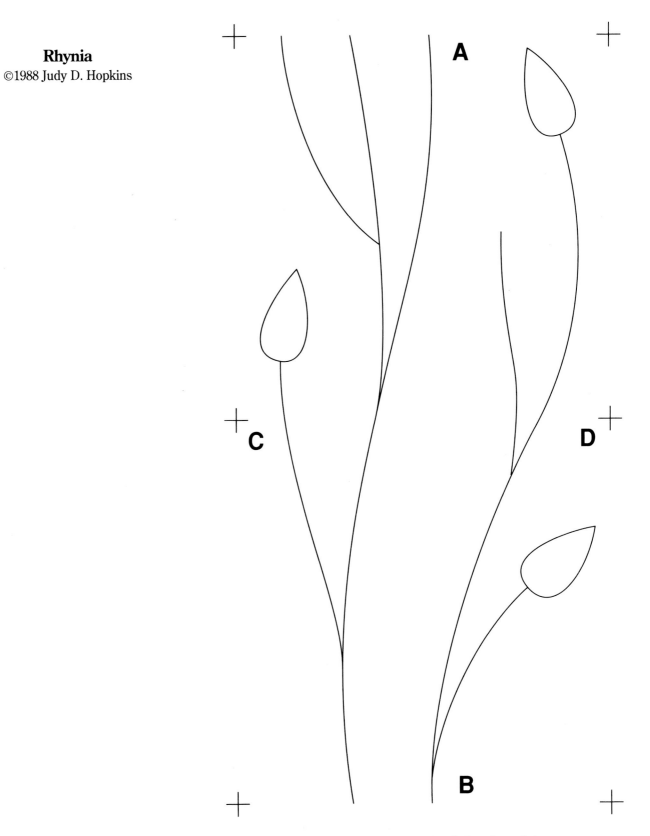

This design is based on a fossil plant form. It is most
effective repeated in a vertical half-drop format,
as shown in the repeat sketch.

Filigree
©1991 Judy D. Hopkins

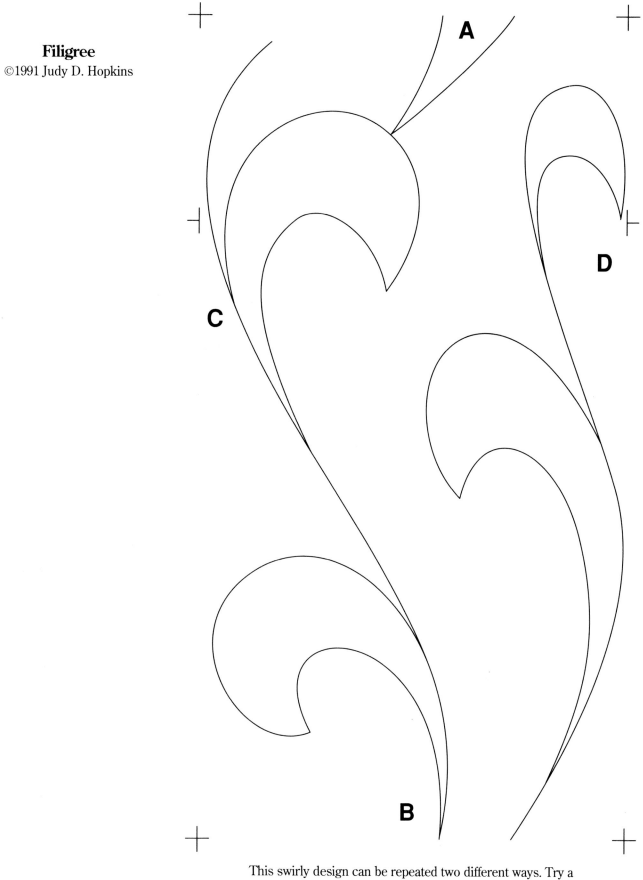

This swirly design can be repeated two different ways. Try a
quarter-drop, as shown in the repeat sketch, or use the "B"
end as the top of the pattern for alternate rows.

THAT PATCHWORK PLACE PUBLICATIONS AND PRODUCTS

The Americana Collection
    by Nancy Southerland-Holmes
    Liberty Eagle   *Old Glory*
    Stars and Stripes   *Uncle Sam*
Angelsong by Joan Vibert
Angle Antics by Mary Hickey
Appliqué Borders: An Added Grace
    by Jeana Kimball
Baby Quilts from Grandma by Carolann M. Palmer
Back to Square One by Nancy J. Martin
A Banner Year by Nancy J. Martin
Basket Garden by Mary Hickey
Blockbuster Quilts by Margaret J. Miller
Calendar Quilts by Joan Hanson
Cathedral Window: A Fresh Look
    by Nancy J. Martin
Christmas Memories—A Folk Art Celebration
    by Nancy J. Martin
Copy Art for Quilters by Nancy J. Martin
Country Threads by Connie Tesene and Mary
    Tendall
Even More by Trudie Hughes
Fantasy Flowers: Pieced Flowers for Quilters
    by Doreen Cronkite Burbank
Feathered Star Sampler by Marsha McCloskey
Fit To Be Tied by Judy Hopkins
Five- and Seven-Patch Blocks & Quilts for the
    ScrapSaver™ by Judy Hopkins
Four-Patch Blocks & Quilts for the ScrapSaver™
    by Judy Hopkins
Handmade Quilts by Mimi Dietrich
Happy Endings—Finishing the Edges of Your Quilt
    by Mimi Dietrich
Holiday Happenings by Christal Carter
Home for Christmas by Nancy J. Martin and
    Sharon Stanley
In the Beginning by Sharon Evans Yenter
Lessons in Machine Piecing by Marsha McCloskey
Little By Little: Quilts in Miniature
    by Mary Hickey
More Template-Free™ *Quiltmaking*
    by Trudie Hughes
My Mother's Quilts: Designs from the Thirties
    by Sara Nephew
Nifty Ninepatches by Carolann M. Palmer

Nine-Patch Blocks & Quilts for the ScrapSaver™
    by Judy Hopkins
Not Just Quilts by Jo Parrott
Ocean Waves by Marsha McCloskey and
    Nancy J. Martin
One-of-a-Kind Quilts by Judy Hopkins
On to Square Two by Marsha McCloskey
Pineapple Passion by Nancy Smith and
    Lynda Milligan
Quilts to Share by Janet Kime
Red and Green: An Appliqué Tradition
    by Jeana Kimball
Reflections of Baltimore by Jeana Kimball
Scrap Happy by Sally Schneider
Shortcuts: A Concise Guide to Metric Rotary Cutting
    by Donna Lynn Thomas
Shortcuts: A Concise Guide to Rotary Cutting
    by Donna Lynn Thomas
Small Talk by Donna Lynn Thomas
Stars and Stepping Stones by Marsha McCloskey
Tea Party Time: Romantic Quilts & Tasty Tidbits
    by Nancy J. Martin
Template-Free™ *Quiltmaking* by Trudie Hughes
Template-Free™ *Quilts and Borders*
    by Trudie Hughes
Threads of Time by Nancy J. Martin
Women and Their Quilts
    by Nancyann Johanson Twelker

Tools	**Video**
6" Bias Square®	Shortcuts to America's
8" Bias Square®	Best-Loved Quilts
Metric Bias Square®	
BiRangle™	
Pineapple Rule	
Rotary Mate™	
Rotary Rule™	
ScrapSaver™	

Many titles are available at your local quilt shop.
For more information, send $2 for a color catalog
to That Patchwork Place, Inc., PO Box 118,
Bothell, WA 98041-0118.